MW01592567

LEGENDARY

Tall Tales and How to Become One

Keith G. Alderman

CONTENTS

Preface   9

Part 1: Desiring Legends   15

Part 2: Earning Legends   41

Part 3: Legend Character   63

Part 4: No One Can Steal Your Destiny   99

Part 5: Even if It's the Last Thing We Do   133

Notes   179

Appendices   185

THANKS

J. Marvin Alderman for the decades of stories, lessons and memories, and that three hour Starbucks breakfast where you made sense out of everything.

Betty and Gene Coulter for meeting with me and giving every great memory, tying off loose ends, confirming my suspicions, and blessing my kids with popsicles. You are both *legends*.

Faye Alderman-Causey and Leland "*Granddaddy*" Alderman for the love, stories and adventures in my childhood.

Carlia Alderman for championing and supporting me in this journey and allowing me to test regularly my wildness to see if there is bravery behind it.

PREFACE

I suspect that at the root and in the strongest ambitions of our human hearts are the proddings and purposefulness to have a life of meaning and legend. We were designed to adore God and leave behind a legacy. But of course, our hope for a life of *"meaning"* gets muddy when we judge it without the factors of a mere life of worship and love. Those two elements are the qualifications required for making us legends in God's eyes.

But in our *own* eyes do we come up short. We wear our missteps and mistakes on our shoulders like heavy weights keeping us at the floor of an ocean of historical mistakes. If we are to live with the right mind, hope, and confidence God has designed us to obtain, we must discover what makes us legends here on earth.

What *naturally* propels us, and what *supernatural* propellant is behind it? Perhaps it's merely a selfish desire to be *"recognized"*. Or perhaps, that passion is God's own spiritual unctioning that propels us toward doing more, meaning more, and accomplishing greater things, and the reaction of it, too, would make *Him* known.

I was a ten-year-old, the first time I heard the stories and *Tall Tales* outlined in this book. The story of my mighty great-grandfather Marvin Daniel Alderman. A man that carried pride and bravery like a badge on his shoulder. He was a hero.

We love our hero stories. Stories of men and women who refuse to sway by fear or impossibility; the people who reside in adventure. But something happens to us when we age. Regret, abandonment and rejection pervert our innocence. Our fictional heroes tell us to dream big, whilst our earthly leaders tell us to "grow up" and "gauge ourselves properly".

What happened to *"nothing is impossible"?*

What happened to the notion that we can *"be anything"* we desire?

When we age, we discover that our heroes in life are flawed and broken; some worse than us. And if we are too quick to learn their error, instead of their grace, we will miss the opportunity to grow into someone else's hero one day. Thus, the majority of us live lives never truly capable of it.

What would it be like to live a life that someone else envied? When we imagine that, it tempts us to conjure up an idea that someone would only listen to us if we were wealthy and on a billboard. But any child will tell you they do not find their heroes in millionaires; they find them in *Luke Skywalker, Indiana Jones* and *Wonder Woman*. Men and women wealthy in character and strength, as opposed to stature and fame.

What would it take for you to seek a life that a child looks at in awe? What would it cost you? And where would you even start in a world full of letdowns and ambiguity?

This is the message of my book. One that I have desired to write since I started hearing about the great Marvin Daniel Alderman. In his *Tall Tales* are the stuff of Legend and that which will make us one.

The stories of my great-grandfather are ones that inspire and influence both with their wild eccentricities and painful honesty. In one hundred years, these stories were never officially written, until now; thus, have only ever been whimsically transposed through generations of storytellers and listeners. This leaves a margin of error. Nonetheless, nearly 100% of what you are about to read is entirely true; though some names, dates and clothing may be inaccurate, the occurrences, words, and happenings are entirely authentic.

—K.G.A.

For J. Marvin, Leland and Marvin

PART 1:
Desiring Legends

"The safest road to Hell is the gradual one—
the gentle slope, soft underfoot,
without sudden turnings,
without milestones, without signposts."
- C.S. Lewis

i. the creature from the black lagoon

The hot Florida summer sun pierced through the long black limbs of the canopy like a thousand strong fingers crawling across the swampy ground and cypress knees. Cicadas and honeybees sang their vibrating songs in anthem. Squirrels danced and chased one another. Fluttering leaves, shuddering in the breeze, mimicked a green ocean wave standing upright along the riverbank.

Out of the black underbelly of the forest, came two silhouette figures, slowly trudging through the muddy slop. One carried a ten-foot piece of rebar across his shoulder; the other held a .22 rifle draped across his forearm. Their shoes sloshed in the mud, sinking ankle-deep into the muck as they approached the edge of the river. The older handsome brother stared at the stagnant black water. He jabbed the rebar at the end of the bank. It stuttered in his hands, hitting dry ground only a few inches below the mud.

He edged himself a few yards down the bank and stabbed at it again. It, too, hit solid ground below the mud. The two men quietly continued their way down the river, stopping to jab at it every few yards. Finally, the rod appeased the young man when it cut through the bank and sunk half its length into the ground.

Without a word, the young man stepped slowly into the black water, using the rebar to balance himself. The cold shocking river rose up around his belly and torso, stopping just above the chest. He bobbed in the water, positioning his pole about his waist. He made slow methodical jabs under the riverbank into the large cavern the pole had discovered.

Maneuvering about the edges and crooks of cypress roots and boulders, his pole hit the belly of a beast that came rushing out, straight at his legs, taking him off his feet. Out of the water came the head of a ten-foot alligator. The man and monster stared into one another's eyes, challenging each to flinch.

"Shoot him, Roy," the young man said flatly.

On the bank, Marvin Alderman's younger brother Roy was holding his .22 rifle. He already had the gun up and aimed at the beast. He fired a single shot at the back of the alligator's eye, only three feet from Marvin's face.

The gator went berserk, flipping its body into a death roll, throwing waves and mud everywhere. Marvin was already under the water, diving away from the animal. He came up out of the water a few yards from the affair. He awkwardly laughed and moaned as he pulled himself out next to his brother.

Roy was still aiming at the water, slowly settling down. The two men waited patiently, their eyes fixed on the gator hole. After a few moments, a large yellow belly rose out of the water. The two laughed and jumped in the water, hauling in their bounty.

"That's a new one for the stories." Marvin exclaimed with a smile on his face, grabbing the massive tail and pulling with all his might.

"That's a stupid one for our grandchildren," Roy replied.

In their short lives, they had cleared dozens of gator holes in the same exact manner. But today, Marvin stared down the barrel of nature's gun. Today, he looked face-to-face with what monsters' eyes carry; and today he walked away the victor. There was no shame in him. There was no panic or fear. There were resolve and response. Today, the monster lost and bravery won.

ii. legendary

"Monsters aren't as scary
if you start shining lights on them."
- Wyatt Cenac

As evening came, Jesus looked upon the water and said to his disciples, "Let's cross to the other side of the lake."[1]

When his disciples, of whom many were fishermen, entered their vessel, they nearly saw the other side of the Sea of Galilee, just over eight miles away. Undoubtedly, they read the sky above; they knew a storm was brewing. Nonetheless, they set out on the boat with Jesus, because He commanded them.

Soon as just they knew it would, a fierce storm came upon them. "Portside!" Peter screamed at James.

"—Brace yourselves!" Another wave came crashing over the side of the small ship.

With high waves breaking over the bow, the boat began to fill with water. It fought its way up the torrential waves and came raging down the other side. The greatest of fishermen feared for their lives; today was the day they would see death face-to-face and lose.

Peter held onto the side of the boat with whatever last muster of faith he had, believing they would get to the other side because the

Master told them to go. John couldn't take it any longer. He rushed to Jesus' sleeping side.

"Teacher," he exclaimed. "Don't you even care that we're going to drown?"

Jesus, looking him in the eyes, smiled. He rose to his feet and rebuked the wind, "Silence! Be still!"

Suddenly the wind stopped, the waves dissolved, the stars shone, and there was a great calm.

The disciples looked about each other, awkwardly wondering what to say and do next.

"Why are you afraid?" Jesus looking at them, asked. "Do you still have no faith?"

On the other side of the Sea of Galilee sat a man, demon-possessed by countless spirits. He was a man that all of Decapolis knew well and feared, so powerful and manic in his demon-possession that he often chewed himself from his chains, attached to the mountainside.[2]

When Jesus approached him, the demons writhed in fear and torment, screaming for the man of God to let them be. At this, Jesus commanded the demons out of the man and freed his life forever. When the man came to his senses, he fell at Jesus' feet and begged for the allowance to follow and serve Him. He bowed before the Man who saved his life and devoted his life to Him.

But Jesus did something peculiar.

Regularly, Jesus would accept the entreaty of people to follow; we frequently see Jesus accepting them.[3] The only people that He didn't, were those that chose to walk away after having received the revelation of it being such a hard life.[4] Here, we see a man with nothing, ready to follow for the rest of his life, *but Jesus refuses him*, encouraging the man to return home and tell everyone of what happened to him.[5] And then Jesus and His disciples return to their boat and cross back to the other side of the sea.

Part of me knows that Peter, James and John would have been dumbfounded, and a bit frustrated, for lack of a better term. These men risked their lives at the hand of a hurricane, dispirited by their so-called lack of faith, and all to only see one man tied up on the side of a cliff set free from demon-possession and then refused to join them. They witnessed countless demon-possessed men and women set free. Why was this man worth the effort of their lives?

But He was worth it to Jesus. And the fruit of the man's changed life was invaluable.

We don't know how long it took for Jesus and the disciples to return to Decapolis. It may have been a few weeks. It may have been months or a year. Regardless, upon Jesus' return to this region[6], a company of people eagerly awaited the Savior of the demoniac and what He had to bring them. In the Gospel of Mark, Chapter Eight we witness Him perform one of His greatest miracles, feeding four thousand men with only seven loaves of bread in His hands.[7]

When Jesus looks at a man or woman, chained to the cliff-side and run over by demonic forces, His heart moves with compassion, enough to cross a storm of Hell. We may not see the fruit of it for a long time to come. But when it comes, it comes with a flurry of people's lives changed. That demoniac, set free, went home, and his notoriety gave him the ability to preach and proclaim the goodness of Jesus, so much so that well over 10,000 individuals* were waiting for the day of Jesus' return.

---

*men plus wives and children

21

And it started with Jesus looking at a storm with the disciples, and saying, "Let's cross to the other side of the lake." And those men choosing to believe in Him, instead of their circumstances.

There are creatures that lurk in the dark shadows of this world; ones far more powerful than a ten-foot alligator. And often life calls us to climb into the water with nothing but a piece of rebar to draw them out. And many times, we find ourselves face-to-face with the monster when it chooses to come out. In those moments, we can choose to panic, run, or walk away from our faith. Or we can simply call out for our Savior, and He will calm the waves and get us to the other side. Or like my great-grandfather said to his brother, "Shoot him, Roy."

On the other side of your greatest threat is your greatest fruit. But you must choose to get in the boat and cross to the other side of it. You must fight through fear of death and call upon the name of the Lord. And when it doesn't seem like it was worth it at all, rest assured that the disciples felt that way often, only to be surprised by 4,000 families on the hillside, hungry and waiting.

iii. simply here

"People intoxicate themselves with work
so they won't see how they really are."
                                        - Aldous Huxley

When I was eight years old, I stood at the edge of my street in Cocoa, Florida, listening to my father describe a new movie out that summer: *Braveheart.*[8] Excitedly, he described the premise of the hero of Scotland, and that *the action hero* Mel Gibson was acting and directing it. My family always took our movie-watching experiences very seriously, and we anticipated this movie to be something of a truly great status.

William Wallace was a legend that none of us knew about. But we knew that if he was a legend, he was worth talking about. It was promised that he sliced kings in half, fought for the weak, and said amazing quotes about all men dying but only a few really living. That fiery passion of heroism, justice and desire for change made him a man worth following, dying for, and telling his story.

Something has always been inside of God's children, whether or not we bury it away with age and regret. It is birthed there with us when the heavens first breathed life into our lungs. It is formed inside of us while we were yet in our mother's wombs. Our Sunday school classes inspire it as we learn about the heroes of our past.

Every boy and girl wants to be like David when he fought a lion with his bare hands. We hope to make a boat so grand that all the animals of the earth could fit upon it, and sail away like Noah. We hope, like Samson did, to tear down the walls of the Philistine's temple with the push of our hands; to save an entire race like Esther; to sleep with lions like Daniel; chosen to carry the Savior of the world like Mary.

These are the stories our Sunday School teachers give us, not necessarily because they are the most important stories for young children to learn, but because our teachers learned long ago, that these are the stories children want to hear.

It's only after we grow up and let failure determine our desire, that we become like Zacchaeus, the rich, famous, small and suffering. It's in our old age that men desire to be handsome, tall and rich like the selfish and insecure King Saul. But at our beginning, in the innocent and free imagination of a child and his or her ambition, is the birth of a desire to be something like the man swallowed by a fish that lived to tell the tale, though nothing else was ever said about him.

DESIRING LEGENDS

Human beings know deep down inside that there is something greater than the success of a business deal or paycheck. We don't want to be successful in life. We want to be *legends* of life, with a thousand men and women telling our story millennia from now.

But that hunger for a legendary life slowly dissolves with age. It leaves us with great regret when we discover we are not very special. In fact, someone else has *already done it*, and someone else has *already seen it*.

Today is nothing more than our day to make it through. Not to change the status quo or see the salvation of a thousand orphans. No, today is a day where men and women are asked in the supermarket, by the lady across the counter, "How are you doing?" and they reply: *"I'm here."*

When my great-grandfather Marvin Alderman would scout through the woods of Central Florida, he oftentimes carried nothing more than a .22 pistol, shooting snakes and potentially dangerous pests he came across. The .22 has always been small, but accurate. Not very powerful, but deadly with the right marksman. Marvin was a force to be reckoned with, though he was not easily agitated or excitable.

In the early 1900s, somewhere in the woods of DeSota County, Florida, Marvin searched for sign of game and wildlife. He crunched his way through the thickets and brambles, looking at every footprint and scratch, discovering where the game was moving. He could be out hunting deer, hog, alligator, snake, squirrel, or anything else worth a pelt or meal.

He turned round a bend and stumbled upon a large adult black bear, not 30 feet from him. The animal was immediately disturbed. Marvin dug his feet into the ground, pulling his sidearm. The piddly .22 was not much against a full-grown 500-pound animal, but he pointed his minuscule weapon at him, nonetheless. When the bear charged, Marvin started firing.

The .22 bullet is not powerful enough to penetrate the skull of a bear. Thankfully, there are nine bullets in a .22 revolver. It took all nine at the center of the bear's skull to put the animal down. Every shot hit its mark; each cracking a little more into the skull of the animal. It fell with a powerful thud at his feet.

"I'm here." Marvin exhaled slowly, shaken, but not stirred.

But this *here* was not an earthly place; this *here* was full of purpose and action. This day was one that would be told around fireplaces and car rides for decades to come. The day that Marvin killed a full-grown black bear with nothing more than a .22 pistol. The day that a man wouldn't run from death, but stood his ground and conquered it.

iv. your matter

*"If I find in myself a desire
which no experience in this world can satisfy,
the most probable explanation
is that I was made for another world."*
- C. S. Lewis

"Don't be ridiculous!" King Saul shouted at the boy, arrogant enough to believe he could take on the giant and save the Israelites. For more than forty days, the nine-and-a-half foot Philistine walked out, brandishing his sword and challenging the small and insignificant Israelites. His armor alone weighed more than the boy David.

"There's no way you can fight this Philistine and possibly win!" the King rebuked David. "You're only a boy, and he's been a man of war since his youth!"

But David persisted. "I have been taking care of my father's sheep and goats. When a lion or a bear comes to steal a lamb from the flock, I go after it with a club and rescue the lamb from its mouth. If the animal turns on me, I catch it by the jaw and club it to death. I have done this to both lions and bears, and I'll do it to this pagan Philistine, too, for he has defied the armies of the living God! The Lord who rescued me from the claws of the lion and the bear will rescue me from the Philistine!"

David knew in his heart, something that no Israelite was willing to understand. He understood who God was and what He was capable of. God had not given him a spirit of fear, but a spirit that belonged to God's power.[9]

God's children weren't created to bow to temptation, fear, or conflict. We were designed to thrive in those moments. *Why then, are we so surprised when they come into our lives?*

If our focus is like David's, no problem or conflict is too great for us. Instead, we are irritated when others are too slow to act upon them. Our fights and conflicts should be natural parts of our lives. It's in the mundane that we should be wary of where our hearts have wandered. In the mundane are Bathsheba's[10] and Uriah's[11]. In the conflict, lies the opportunity for God to do something great.

What's interesting to note is that David credits the Lord for rescuing him from the claws of the lion and the bear, yet we know that David had another reasonable "rescue". In fact, David never had to fight and put his life in danger, to begin with.

It's only in the process of saving his sheep that his life entered peril. On the hillside, while watching the lion approach, he could have fled at any moment. The lion and bear were never there for David; they were there for the sheep. David's character of bravery and action *forced* him to intervene.

Even still, David credits that the lion and bear were after *his* life, and *he* needed saving. In his mind, when the sheep were in danger, he was a victor, whose duty it was to rescue the sheep. He would not let danger and fear overcome his purpose. They were in danger, and it was his duty to save them.

Once, he is incapable of doing it alone, and within the jaws of the bear, he realizes the bear is after *his life*. David walked in two states of mind, constantly; that he was fully capable and fully *incapable* to do anything heroic. He was brave and aware that his bravery rested in God's power.

When walking through our lives, we may come upon 500-pound bears that we never would have found unless we were walking out and searching. It would be tempting to blame the presence of our bears on our "desire for discovery". We say things like, "I should have known better than to try…"

But the bear is the problem, not our wanderlust.

If we blame the presence of our conflict on our determination to discover and grow, we will stop growing altogether. We must understand that bears just come and go in the woods. You were designed in your life to meet conflict and face it head on. You were made to fight it, no matter what, and when the bear has its mouth around your neck, to know that God will rescue you, just as He rescued David on the hillside.

With this perspective, we are apter running *toward* conflict, approaching it with the knowledge that God has given us power, love and a sound mind; able to stand, move with compassion, and think clearly. If, and when, we know that God is for us, nothing can be against us[12], and that we are victorious[13], regardless of the outcome, we will stand our ground, firing as many shots as it takes to bring down the charging beast.

But this perspective is lost when we think our purpose on earth is nothing more than to make it *through* it. I see the everyday Christian believing one of two things regarding their purpose here on earth. Either they stand on a borderline-narcissistic ideal that they will be God's chosen vessel to reach the entire world and stand as heaven's celebrity, or believe that life is really not about them and won't amount to much at all. Both are rooted in the godly characteristics of bravery and humility. But both become dangerously out of sorts when perspective is lost.

Let's look at the exaggerated stereotypes of each characteristic, to avoid the inadvertent jabs you and I may feel otherwise. The brave hero of today longs for immediate satisfaction, ready to be lifted on the shoulders of a nation like David was. Yet he refuses to conquer his small fights on a daily basis. He dreams big about slaying giants and conquering entire countries, but refuses to do any daily work on the hillside where no one is watching.

In reality, David became king on the hillside, not on the battlefield. His victory of the bear determined his victory of the giant. Real legends are written by your character, not by your fame.

The other person sits on his hands with his face pointed at the ground, acting as though he never dreamed a dream of worth and power. He has convinced himself that he must live a humble and meaningless life if he is to do God's work. The very thought of fighting real battles terrifies him because he has never looked at himself as a fighter. He knows that he is a *victor* because that's what God told him. But that's different from being a *fighter*. In fact, he knows that people aren't meant to make a powerful difference anymore. That's just what we tell our children. Legends have become fairy-tales.

Faith and action bring victory. And victory brings unwavering faith and action. It was David's history of victory that made him arrogant in his faith—the arrogance to stand before a king and declare that he would be more than able to defeat a ten-foot swordsman. That arrogance was earned, and rooted in the knowledge of the power of God. It doesn't come until you have purposed in your heart to defeat the little battles before the big ones. And likewise, you are meant to defeat the little battles before the big ones, but that doesn't mean you aren't meant to still accomplish the big ones.

The truth is that we find ourselves constantly walking in and out of those two extremes, scared of our own pride and irritated by our own lack of ambition. It's in the understanding that our pride must be rooted in God's power and our ambition must be rooted in Jesus' love that we find our purpose and the divine tension we are meant to tread upon. It's here we find our *meaning*.

In order to get to the place of *mattering*, our first understanding must be that we do, in fact, *matter*. We cannot do something worthwhile unless we realize, again, that we are meant to do something worthwhile. When I hear sixty-year-old men and women say they are embarrassed to ask a thirty-year-old couple for advice, my heart breaks. Not because they have missed their opportunity or purpose, but because they have missed God's heart toward them.

Your status on planet earth may be determined by your age or your experience, but your status in Heaven is determined by your heart and action. Start dreaming again and then start chasing the dream.

We were made to make legends. It is put in us. And each of our lives are meant to be recounted by the children beyond us, around fireplaces and park benches, in order to inspire them to dream again and express the majesty of who God is. We cannot simply be "here" on earth. We must be *Heaven here on earth*. And in that redirection of our focus and purpose, we will be legends worth telling.

v. the two pennies

"The boundaries which divide Life from Death
are at best shadowy and vague. Who shall say where the one ends,
and the other begins?"

- Edgar Allan Poe

Tuesday afternoon, word got round to Reverend Marvin that Sister Margaret was at death's doorstop and the family needed prayer. He rolled up his white cuffed sleeves and rushed to her home, speeding down the long dirt road, a plume of dust and smoke behind him. The sun blazed, the birds chirped, and the street was silent as he stepped out of his truck. He knew before he rapped the door she was already gone.

Brother Justus opened the door with dried tears on his cheeks.

"Come on in, Reverend," he welcomed him miserably.

Marvin looked about the room without a word as he took into account. There, in the front room, in the middle of the floor, lay Margaret. She had pennies on her eyelids, so the rigor mortis wouldn't force her eyes open. Her three children sat on the floor next to her, staring, crying and confused.

Justus started recanting what had happened to his bride, her sickness growing worse to worst in moments. Marvin listened half-heartedly as he stared frustrated and heartbroken at the three children and this man who was held together by sticks in front of him. The man couldn't take it any longer, he broke down and grabbed hold of Marvin crying.

"This isn't right," Marvin said under his breath. "God…this isn't right."

Marvin taught at his church a fiery kind of faith about God. They believed that acting unholy or with unholy people could damage your righteousness; if you died while backslidden you could lose salvation and go to Hell. Death was a normal part of life and rarely was disease looked at like an attack from the Enemy. It's not that he believed God sent death to people. But more death just came at any moment, and "you best hurry up and get straight with God before you meet Him".

Regardless of all that, righteous indignation came over Marvin at that moment. He looked at this man and his three kids and knew that God didn't kill this woman. He knew that her destiny was to live longer and raise these children.

At that moment, he pushed Justus off his shoulder and walked over to the corpse on the living room floor.

"This isn't right," he shouted at the woman. "Lady, get up! In the name of Jesus, get up!"

Her eyes popped open and her spirit returned, sucking the air out of the room. The children stared in disbelief, as the two pennies fell from their mother's eyes and rolled under the living room couch. Margaret stood up and immediately began preparing dinner for their guest.

vi. what makes a legend worth telling

*"Jump, and you will find out
how to unfold your wings as you fall."*
- Ray Bradbury

The man hurriedly pushed and shoved his way through the crowd of people. Sweat ran down his face in exhaustion and desperation. His entourage followed quickly behind, their master running away in a panic.

The man finally made his way through the crowd to the Teacher. "Please, please!" He desperately cried as he fell down to the ground. "My daughter. She is sick and dying. You must see her."

"Jairus!"[14] A man from the back of the crowd hollered at him.

Jairus turned his attention from the Messiah and looked at his servant, not more than 50 meters from him. "Jairus," the servant hollered again. "Your daughter is dead!" Jairus' face fell sullen and defeated.

The servant closed the gap between the two men. He put his hand on his master's shoulder, saying, "She's dead, Jairus. There's no use bothering the Teacher now."

Jesus had just returned from Decapolis, on the other side of the Sea of Galilee where He had met a man chained to the rock and set him free from a legion of demons. He was tired and smelled of fish. He, too, put his hand on Jairus' collar, turning him toward Himself again. "Don't be afraid," He said, "just have faith."

Fear is the embodiment of a spirit coming to hinder, hurt or distract you. *Being afraid* is the manifested response to that hindering distraction. The difference between *having fear* and *being afraid* is: one is out of our control; the other is our response and furthermore acquisition of that fear.

I use the term *"have fear"* only because it is the phrase we most commonly understand. But it's not my intent to paint the picture that we *have* this Spirit, in the same manner, we obtain or own something. Instead, it would be better to imagine you *have* the spirit of fear, in the same manner, you *have* a bird sitting on your head. It's true that it is on your person, but by no means do you desire it or would allow it to perch much more than the amount of time it took you to realize it was sitting atop your noggin. *Being afraid* is the manifestation of having fear. It's the act of letting the bird make a nest and call your head home.

You can *have* fear because it comes and attacks you, causing your fear. But you never have to *be afraid.* That is the choice or allowance of that fear in your heart. Instead, when you *have fear*, you must do what Jesus demanded Jairus do: Look at him and just *have faith,* therefore letting yourself *become faithful.*

Jairus' desperation yielded his fear to the faith in the Messiah. Jairus was a leader of the local synagogue; therefore, this was something he was not keen to do. In fact, the synagogue would look down on him for having turned to Jesus for help at all. He could lose his title, or worse, imprisoned or stoned for this act of heresy. Yet, because he had nowhere left to turn, he quickly let go of the fear of what the synagogue, men, or Jerusalem may do or think of him, and instead only focused on his daughter's life. He had faith in turning to Jesus in order to save his daughter. Faith far outweighed any fear in or of his life. Upon their first meeting, Jesus saw this faith in him.

But the fear would not let up on Jairus. The almost immediate news of his daughter already being dead was reported to him. Now, like a rushing wind, the feelings of desperation are replaced by despondency. Fear comes with an electric jolt, agitating our hearts, but grief comes with a knife in the ribcage, up into the lungs where it's hard to breathe. Jairus was speechless and afraid.

But Jesus knew he had faith inside of him. And He wouldn't let Jairus' pain diminish his power. He stops Jairus from speaking and tells him to remember that he believes.

When Jesus arrived at Jairus' home with him, the place was a circus. People gathered inside, weeping and wailing for the death of the master's daughter. But few gathered in honor, rather in the obligatory mourning of an official's loss.

"Why are you all weeping?" Jesus addresses their parade. "The girl is not dead. She is only sleeping."

In an instant, the tension breaks in the crowd of sycophants, as they laugh and jeer at the fool before them. "Who is this man?" They mock. "He doesn't know what he speaks of. He must be drunk."

Jesus turns to Jairus again. "Put everyone out." He says. "Only come inside with me, your wife, and my three disciples."

When Jesus stood before the little girl, he smiled, knowing this was not God's plan. I can imagine him looking at Jairus and encouraging his faith that this was not right and needed to change.

"Little girl," He demands. "Get up!"

At that, the little girl breathed heavily, sucking the air out of the room. Jairus and his wife grabbed their daughter, crying in joyful disbelief.

The heart of the Messiah is for His children to know the Father, and that the Father loves them. Our faith activates the miraculous, whether or not we fully understand it. And it was Jairus' desperate faith that pushed him beyond fear, to ask for Jesus' help. It was Jesus' faithful command that pulled Jairus beyond the fear of his daughter's reported death into the faith of the miraculous. And all of that faith led to the redemption of the little girl.

"Give her something to eat," Jesus says.

Inside the bland and dry Tuesday afternoons of our lives, God is willing to move. And He is not looking for perfect beings to move upon. My great-grandfather's view of God was not perfect, nor was his understanding of healing sound. But on the afternoon he raised Margaret from the dead, the Spirit of God's anger toward death moved his heart. And it only took him acting upon that movement, that he was able to witness an incredible miracle.

Your limited understanding of the Word of God only limits your ability to believe Him for what it says. It does not limit *Him*.

Oftentimes in their ignorance, *"new"* Christians see more miracles than those with Masters of Theology, simply because they refuse to doubt. Our experience tells us that miracles can't happen; the Word of God tells us something different.

No matter what life looks like, I cannot let experience determine my faith but must push my experiences to meet my faith. God designed us to believe for His will. And any time our experiences don't meet that mark, we need to live in the awkward and terrible tension of pushing our experiences up to a higher standard. When we die believing for something impossible, is when we die at God's best.

And in that pushing and believing is where we find our purpose. It is not to leave a legacy of fame and fortune, but stories of inspiration that radically and intimately changed the history of someone else's eternity forever.

Eternity is where my legacy is birthed. Everything before that, trying to push, pull, bite and fight to survive is foolhardy. Because I wasn't meant to survive; I was meant to let go. Legends never die. But the people behind them do. So in that understanding, hopefully, we can put aside the childish ideal that life is about *us*, and understand that the greatest legacy we will have, is the one that is told after we are dead.

You weren't meant to change history. You were meant to create it. Not for your gain, but for the gain of God's children. And nothing can deter that choice of creating legends except you. Your knowledge, upbringing or season don't determine your story. Only what you choose to do with them, *right now*, does.

In the choice and desire to be a *legend*, we will face monsters, dig them out from the holes they hide in, stand our ground against the Enemy, and rescue the dead from death. And our children's children will be the ones passing our stories along, to inspire and create history again.

That's what makes a legend worth telling.

vii. going one more time

"It's not the size of the dog in the fight,
it's the size of the fight in the dog."
- Mark Twain

God doesn't call the special. He calls the crazy.

Growing up, I fantasized that the men Jesus chose to disciple and walk with were his childhood friends; men that He knew well for His entire life. We only see a few glimpses into how He asked these men to walk with Him, and most are nothing more than the account that these men suddenly started walking with Him. We read a few words here and there about Jesus requesting others to "come follow [Him]" and see their acceptance, but we don't read much more about it.

The more I learn how Jesus chooses those He's going to do ministry with, the more I realize He's not looking for a specific *individual*; He's looking for a specific *type*. There are precisely unremarkable tales of men saying yes to following Jesus, because these men were *precisely unremarkable*. Hence, we see little of the story itself and even less of their lives beforehand. This implies that there must have been plenty of other *unremarkable* people whom Jesus asked as well, who denied His invitation (think of the young rich ruler, for example).

It wasn't the *person* whom Jesus desired; it was the *personality* that He craved. Now, don't misinterpret my meaning to think that Jesus isn't going to let everyone follow Him. In fact, His invitation was often and eager, and many followed Him by calling Him

Messiah and Lord. But only a few men were the ones crazy enough to follow under the wildest circumstances, and thus, were the ones that became legends.

When I refer to Jesus desiring a specific *type of person*, I am only referring to His will to create powerful testimonies and stories in history with *those people*. He desires every human as his children and followers, and just as much for everyone to have this personality, whether or not they have it today. But it is our limitations we put on ourselves that will determine or diminish the stories we have passed down behind us. Thereby, many will remain *ordinary*, though that doesn't mean God loves them less. The disciples, indeed, were the ones that left everything and followed Jesus *immediately*.

Along the Sea of Galilee, early in the morning, Jesus walked with a group of people who were eagerly waiting to hear from Him. The party was so large that he needed to steal a boat and set out into the water to speak clearly for all to hear.

I live in a fishing community where nearly everyone has fished at some point in their lives, but few have fished all night. And even fewer have fished all night for their occupation. And even fewer still have fished all night for their occupation and caught *nothing*. The men I know that fish all night are a certain sort of person. They are gruff, rough and pissed when they set to work for no reason. Regardless, rarely do they experience an evening of *nothing*.

I recall a time that Peter Deeks, a camera operator serving on our church production team, blessed me with a day fishing trip with his son in Sebastian Inlet, Florida. Peter Deeks Jr. took my father, friend Neil, and myself out on a trip that normally would have cost a few hundred dollars just for an hour of fishing with him. When we set out on the boat, early in the morning, I understood that we would catch some good fish, but had no idea how talented Peter really was.

Not fifteen minutes into our trip, Peter stopped the boat and encouraged me to cast my rod to an area of the water only ten yards from us. In less than ten seconds, I was reeling in a 31-inch gator trout. Peter wasn't a professional; he was a god. It is rare that he ever experiences a day without a trophy fish; it is even rarer that he would experience a day of *no* fish.

But this was Peter's (the disciple) dilemma. He was a man that needed a certain amount of fish in order to survive—not just for himself, but for the community. And he spent the entire night, toiling and struggling to get just *one* fish worth taking in.

As he crouched at the bank of the Sea of Galilee, cleaning his nets, exhausted and ready to go home and rest, he looked up to see the Man Jesus getting in his boat and setting out to speak to a crowd of people. I can only imagine it frustrated him, as it would me.

When Jesus finished speaking, he addressed Peter, "Now go out where it is deeper, and let down your nets to catch some fish." This was the defining moment for Peter and his walk with Jesus. Amidst exhaustion, frustration, anger and shame, he obeyed Jesus, if not, at the least, a little reluctantly. "Master," Simon replied, "We worked hard all last night and didn't catch a thing. But if you say so, I'll let the net down again."

They set out the boat. Paddle after paddle, stroke after stroke, they took the boat into the deep. With all left in them, they threw the net into the sea. Their splintered and calloused hands gripped the ropes and pulled. But this time their net was so full of fish it tore.

When they pulled into shore, Peter fell to Jesus' feet. "Oh, Lord," he said, "please leave me. I'm such a sinful man." His doubt and stubborn acquiesce filled his heart with shame. How could he ever have second-guessed the Son of Man?

But this was the exact character Jesus was searching for. He didn't need the talented, brave or intelligent. He needed the foolish, stubborn and penitent. Because behind that foolishness rests a natural inclination to go out one more time upon the water, on the other side of failure after failure, and let down the nets again. Not because he necessarily believed it, but because Jesus commanded him. And his penitence matched his lack of belief.

The character that Jesus craves and knows will change the world is brash and crazy. Of course, it gets tired. Of course, it gets frustrated. But above all else, it obeys and goes out one more time. Jesus isn't looking for "Christians" to change the world. He's looking for those crazy enough to go one more time and send down the nets. God doesn't call the special. He calls the crazy.

PART 2:
Earning Legends

*"Deep into that darkness peering,
long I stood there, wondering, fearing,
doubting, dreaming dreams
no mortal ever dared to dream before."*
                              - Edgar Allan Poe

i. face to face with a monster

Contrary to popular belief, Florida has had winters of extreme cold. Of course, it is rare and only lasts a fortnight. But it happens. The air thins out and activity comes to a stutter. Dry days feel pleasant and heartening. But most days aren't dry; the wet ones create an atmosphere that burns more than it chills. One such winter, Marvin camped in the northern parts of what would become our Everglades. Of course, camping for Marvin and his brother Roy was nothing more than hanging a piece of tarp from a treetop over their blankets, pillows and hunting gear, keeping the rain or hail from bothering their sleep.

In the morning, when waking, Marvin felt a heaviness on his chest unfamiliar to him. Without stirring too much, he removed his blanket to discover a six-foot Eastern Diamondback Rattlesnake coiled up on his chest and torso. America's largest rattlesnake was staring him directly in the face.

Rattlesnakes are, of course, cold-blooded, but have special sensors along the ridge of their upper lip that detect heat. In the middle of the night, the snake used these to find a viable source of heat to warm itself amid the freezing night. That source just happened to be the warm-blooded body of Marvin Alderman.

Though the rattlesnake's intent was nothing sinister, the fact remained that it was a perfect candidate to kill Marvin that morning, if he was to stir violently, angering or startling the reptile. Instead of panicking, Marvin lay still. When Roy woke up, Marvin quietly explained the situation to him and had him leave the premises in case anything were to frighten the snake.

For a full hour, Marvin stared into the lidless eyes of the deadly reptile, as the sun slowly came up. Once the sun satisfied the serpent, it began to crawl off Marvin's chest. Each scale squeezed and drug along his torso, arms and legs as it crawled the length of his entire body. As Marvin felt the final bit of the snake's tail leave him, he stood erect, firmly grasped his shotgun in his hands and blew the head off the monster he slept with; likely about to enjoy eating it for breakfast.

ii. pain activation

*"Whoever is winning at the moment
will always seem to be invincible."*
- George Orwell

"My Father!"

His body shook in grief and despair. His hands trembled in fear. Jesus knelt in the pale moonlight, blanketed by the shadows of the olive trees, empowered by an angel and tormented by the devil, praying to His Father for strength and perseverance. *"If* this cup… cannot be taken away…" He looked up at the night sky, tears in His eyes, sweat pouring down His face. "If there is no other way for this to be done unless I drink it…unless I do this…Your will be done, Father. On earth, as it is in Heaven."[1]

He wiped the blood from his brow, put there by his immense grief and anguish. He plucked leaves from a nearby olive tree to clean his hands and face. These trees would be there for thousands of years to come, preparing oil for many generations. Each olive put through the process of being smashed, ground and left abandoned in a press until every bit of pure oil was extracted from it.

He walked through the garden, discovering He was indeed alone, save the angel still strengthening Him[2], for his friends Peter, James and John had fallen asleep while propped up against a rock and olive tree.

"Couldn't you watch with me even one hour?" he said, shaking Peter awake. "Keep watch and pray, so that you will not give in to temptation. The spirit is willing, but the body is weak."

We have all had times in our lives of excruciating torment. And while they would tempt some of us to measure our pain and grief as greater than another's, more challenging, or life-altering, we must admit that we all have felt and experienced the breathlessness of desperation. The true pain of humans doesn't lie in our hands or senses near as much as in our hearts and minds. There, in our soul, is the place we trap our failures, shame and doubt. In our heart is where give up hope. In our mind is where we tell ourselves we aren't good enough.

But in this pain is the actual motivation, if not *activation*, for your life to have meaning. Those that prepare for greatness use their pain and failure as a catalyst, not an inhibitor. Jesus, in the Garden of Gethsemane, had two spirits speaking to him. An angel of death and an angel of strength. His situation did not change, nor did its inevitable outcome. But his choice of which spirit to walk with determined how He would walk out of the garden.

When Marvin opened his eyes to discover a serpent looking into them, he found an enemy that felt empowered in the night but was destined to die in the morning. Your greatest hurts are only the last-ditch effort of an enemy that wants you to buckle in the night, knowing he will die in the morning.

Choosing to face the monster through the night will lead you to discover that your greatness is not only called by God, but it's called by the Enemy himself. Just as the serpent crawled through the cold night, the enemy is crawling through the world. But his attention is not consumed by those that are cold like him; it is attracted to those that are warm and shining bright. Your pain is evidence of your power. The enemy wouldn't bother with you otherwise. Therefore, your pain is to be the spark to light a fire inside of you.

When desperation comes; when failure rears its ugly head back at you, be strengthened, be encouraged. With the spirit of anguish comes a spirit of empowerment. And both stand beside you, wrestling one another until you decide which you will follow out of the garden.

iii. the greatest punishment

"Our children's children will hear a good story."
- Richard Adams

My grandfather Leland was a Pentecostal minister for his entire adult life. While also a jack-of-all-trades, he pastored any community that would let him; all over New England, parts of New Jersey, California, Tennessee, Alaska, and most of Florida[†]. He

---

[†]including Jacksonville, Lake Wales, Apopka, Plantation Key, Lake Panasoffkee, Ruskin, Boynton Beach and Fellsmere

planted many churches, leaving them to thrive under the community put in place. At most of these churches, he served as the pastor, coordinator and worship leader. He loved every aspect of delivering the Good News to people.

One of Leland's most famous sermons was a story of his childhood with his daddy Marvin. Back then, Leland was a real cuss. He was rebellious and downright ornery, always getting into trouble and never listening to his teachers. His daddy often had to take the belt to his behind, in order to straighten him out.

One such day at school, Leland was busying himself with belligerent and asinine behavior enough to push the teacher beyond his patience. The teacher had Leland retrieve the paddle from the Principal's Office. As Leland returned, he brought it to the teacher's desk, insolently throwing it down.

"Here you go," he said. "What you wanna do with it?"

The teacher didn't reply. He wouldn't acknowledge Leland, who stood confidently with his arms crossed in front of the class. He quietly wrote a letter and asked Leland to take it home immediately to his father. Leland left the room elated, skipping down the hall. Nothing in him desired to give his father that nasty letter; he was simply excited to have the rest of the day off.

Outside and walking down the road, he took a detour through an abandoned gas station. He found an old oil drum and removed the top of it; it was nearly three-quarters full. He stared at the reflection in the black murky oil, swirly and spinning. He let the letter fall from his hand into the drum. He watched it slowly sink into brown rust and milky gray and black water and oil. He waited until every last bit of the white was invisible, then he put the top back on and skipped away.

Shortly thereafter, while wandering through town, he spotted his daddy's car through a row of houses and fences. Something inside him told him that his father must have seen him. Like a deep instinctual voice that told Adam and Eve when God was coming to walk with them in the cool of the day. He was afraid.

He ran off, zigging and zagging through yards, jumping over fences, and disturbing watch-dogs. He knew that his daddy was after him, so he didn't stop zigging around corners of buildings and homes. But one time, his daddy zagged while Leland zigged, and the two of them came face-to-face. Leland knew he was in trouble, and he could see the fire in his daddy's eyes.

"I got a note from your teacher," Marvin calmly said.

"*You found that note?*" Leland was incredulous.

"*What* note?" Marvin smiled curtly.

Leland caught in his father's trickery. He was forced back to the gas station and ordered to dig the letter out. Oil and water sopped down the ends of his little arms and hands.

On the ride back home, he silently scowled in the passenger-seat, cleaning himself off.

"Son," Marvin said. "I've done my best to teach you." He smiled slyly. "I knew I couldn't beat the devil out of you, so I tried to beat him in so far that he wouldn't show." Leland pursed his lips.

"Son," Marvin continued. "I'm a minister in this town. What you do affects how people perceive me, the Church, and God." Marvin sighed frankly in frustration; nothing was getting through.

When the two got home, Leland knew that he was in for it. "Go in the bathroom and wait for me," Marvin said to him. Leland walked into the bathroom, about to receive what he thereafter described as the worst spanking of his life.

He perched on the side of the bathtub, staring at the base of the door, counting the minutes before his daddy was ready to enter. The knob rattled and turned. The door scraped across the linoleum before it thudded against the wall. Leland stared at his daddy's feet.

He heard his father's slow, heavy breath. Inhale. Exhale. "Someone has to pay for what you have done, son."

Leland furrowed his brow, hiding his fear of the pain. But his eyes would betray him when he saw the shirt fall to the ground. He knew that his daddy *must* be mad now. Next, the undershirt fell.

Leland took a heavy breath, closed his eyes, and clenched his jaw. He would not be undone. Then, surprisingly, he felt something nudging him on the forehead. He opened his eyes and looked up. The belt was being held out in front of him. Beyond it, he saw his father staring back at him with tears in his eyes.

"Someone has to take the punishment," Marvin said. "It's *my* fault. So I'll take the punishment. Today, I get the whippin'."

It confused Leland. Fear, pain, betrayal, abandonment all came crashing in on him. It was hard for him to breathe. *Why was his father doing this?* He clenched his jaw again, mustering the courage to steel himself.

"Go on, now," Marvin whispered.

Leland fought back, pushing the belt away. "No, Daddy," he exclaimed. "I can't do that." The two went back and forth. It was all too much for Leland. He fell back into the bathtub. On his knees, he started clawing at the tiled walls, trying to escape the Hell, but his oily hands would only slip and he fell into the bathtub again.

Marvin finally relieved the boy, grabbing him in his arms. "Okay, son," he whispered in his ear. "Okay."

He held him until Leland's panic subsided. Then, with the tip of the belt in his hand, he gently tapped it three times on Leland's shoulder. He kept holding on as his son cried in his arms.

Our Savior Jesus Christ took our punishments on *His* back. He died our deaths for our wages. And through His sacrifice, we could face the Father again.

It was impossible for young Leland to make sense of his father's forfeiture; it drove him mad that he had wickedly broken his father. But true love is a forfeit; love is sacrifice. Likewise, our Father in Heaven gave His Son as the ransom for all of mankind; He fully comprehended the magnitude of our sins and mistakes, greater than any other could, and chose to take the beating.

While we were yet sinners, Christ died for us.[3] While you were yet worthless, Christ had a plan for you; one that exists for greatness. Our greatest critics are ourselves, knowing every detail of our inept and broken lives. Thus, we may never wholly grasp the full extent of what *mercy* and *grace* truly are.[4] We have every lie and sin of our past blocking it.

Regardless, Christ *did* die for us. And it is our individual choice to accept his reward. We will never earn salvation in the same way that you can never earn a gift. Otherwise, it is not a gift—it is a merit badge. God does not see merit; He only sees His children which were all created equal. And being equal, all have fallen into sin and removed themselves from His greatness. But His sacrifice crossed the divide of our sin, only requiring us to cross the bridge back to Him. He willingly took our sins upon Himself.

If your salvation is a choice, then likewise your legend. Choose to have a life of meaning and legacy, with your blood, sweat and tears, much the same as Jesus' in the Garden.[5] For God chooses every moment to look at your sin no more. He has a plan that uses your failures and past to propel you forward, and He refuses to let them hold you back. When we have committed to Him, we quickly understand that He has already committed to us. Stop letting your "lack of qualification" disqualify you from greatness.[6] With Christ, nothing is impossible,[7] except the things that we prohibit ourselves from doing and accomplishing.

iv. the legend of Marbin Aknernab

"Only those who will risk going too far
can possibly find out how far one can go."
                                        - T. S. Eliot

1945.

Our country was on the other side of its Second World War, having witnessed the nobility and bravery mankind can achieve, and the barbaric and demonic. Men were great. Men were evil. But God remained the same.

Leland was eleven years old, filtering through the halls of the University of Miami, searching between the legs of men in fine suits for his father's face. Somehow, he had disconnected from him and panic was settling in. He was a little poor boy from southern Florida that had little business in this large convention of professors and thinkers of theology and religion. He hurried about, pushing legs and grabbing at dresses, fighting his way through the mob.

Finally, he heard the voice of his father, amidst a crowd of white-haired men in suits and ties. "...We have to stop chasing the sinful acts of bad doctrine and start looking at the lost and dying." Marvin stood and spoke at the center of attention. "Jesus said, 'They that are whole need not a physician; but they that are sick.[8]'"

"But what of those that Jesus ran out with a scourge of small cords?[9]" A professor refuted.

"But don't forget—in that, Jesus was dealing with money-changers and those that wanted to sell salvation by means of profit —Which God has never been in the business of paying for salvation but receiving it through Christ Jesus. What we are dealing with is men arguing over which doctrine is correct and which teacher to follow. *Follow Christ.* And stop trying to prove which of you is greatest. Maybe then we can reach the people in need. 'Of these things put them in remembrance, charging them before the Lord that they strive not about words to no profit, but to the subverting of the hearers.'[10]

The educators leaned back on their heels in awe. Who was this man, thick with a southern drawl as he may, that was wowing them for thirty minutes on fundamentals of Christ's teaching and the Old and New Covenants? Marvin would later, in front of his son and many of the university's congregation, be pronounced one of the wisest Christian leaders of their time.

Ironically, he had nothing more than a third-grade education. He could not read and could not write. His inept handwriting was so bad, even *he* could not read it. Eventually, he would purchase a typewriter and teach himself how to type, so that others could understand what he was writing. The first words he ever tried to type, without looking, were his own name. They came out: *Marbin Aknernab.*

Ever since the day he gave his life to Christ in his early twenties, he would walk a half-mile into the woods and sit on a stump with a Bible. On it, God showed him the history of the Bible in the sky. He would pray to God, asking Him to teach him how to read. And each day, for months and months, he would return to that stump, open his Bible, and the Holy Spirit would teach him what it said. He did nothing but worked and read the Word of God every day.

One afternoon, he heard God tell him to go to Frostproof, Florida. He went home and told his wife Mamie that he needed to go, and so they went. When they arrived, Marvin stopped to get a cold drink at a gas station and recognized construction being built nearby.

He approached the group of men working on it and asked what it was for. "It's a brush arbor—For *revival!*" One worker excitedly said. "We believe God is about to start revival here." He looked forlornly down. "—But we don't have a minister yet."

Marvin and Mamie stayed and help them finish the arbor for the next few months. When finished, the Church of God Overseer came to Marvin and asked him to speak. Marvin didn't know what he was getting at or why he thought he should be the one.

"Didn't you get our letter?" The Overseer asked. "You're supposed to be the minister of this place."

Marvin stood and began preaching. He had no history of seminary or proper schooling. But he had the Spirit of God inside of him and the faith to open his mouth. Revival broke out in Frostproof that day, and many were saved. Eight different men declared they would become Church of God ministers out of that one meeting that should never have happened, except a poor illiterate man sitting on a stump in the middle of the woods on the other side of Florida, heard God tell him to go to Frostproof and trust Him.

All throughout his ministry, he had a reputation of turning any church he led into a prosperous and spirit-filled community. He established the largest Church of God in Miami, and was easily one of the greatest ministers the denomination had ever witnessed at that time. Leland told the story again and again of how his father was in the league, if not exceeding that, of professors of theology and God's written Word.

Commitment, determination and the Spirit of God are the ingredients to greatness. God has already supplied His Spirit and will meet all your needs according to Christ's glory. The only other things in the way are your priorities, passion and act of growing up. These are things that formed a poor boy from southern Florida, with nothing more than a third-grade education, into a legend. What are you willing to do and give up for your legacy?

As I already stated, my Granddaddy Leland led his churches by doing *everything* humanly possible in the church. Whatever needed to get done, got done. He coordinated, led worship and preached; many of the songs he played were originals he wrote to Jesus.

He believed that, though he may not have been the most intelligent or gifted speaker of the Christian Church, like that of Billy Graham or Kenneth Hagin, he was capable of out-working anyone. And that mentality sets certain men and women apart from everyone else.

My Granddaddy's acoustic guitar, which he used to write worship songs to Jesus and lead his churches in, hangs over my desk in my office, reminding me that I am the product of generations ahead of me, praying, serving, and loving Jesus with everything in them. Men who chose to chase Jesus, regardless of what they *"knew"* or *"were capable of"*.

They were men who fully understood that God does not make history with the just or able. He uses those that are crazy enough to get out of boats and walk on water when He calls them.[11] He uses those that are crazy enough to let two of God's spies stay in their house while under martial law.[12] He uses those that will proclaim His name, even if it means they get stoned to death, and then get back up again.[13]

Making history is not about reading your Bible and praying. It's about giving *everything* to Him and trusting Him no matter the process. That's why it has to be a choice. Because if it was thrust upon you, it would most likely be a death sentence. Greatness must be attained. He holds His hands out waiting for you to take it, but be sure of what you are about to walk into.

v. fearful following

"The fear of death follows from the fear of life.
A man who lives fully is prepared to die at any time."
                                            - *Mark Twain*

It was the first time 10-year-old Leland ever went hunting at night with Marvin. The father and son were making their way back from their stand, through the cypress swamp, to their camp. Marvin was out in front, led by his headlamp and armed with his rifle and sidearm. Leland kept his eyes on Marvin's legs, his hands in his pockets, silently following, all the while knowing there was plenty out there that could hunt him if he didn't keep up with his daddy.

For over an hour, he listened to his daddy's boots trudge through the mud in front of him, watching the silhouette of his father go up and down against the terrain, the light dancing around the black forest, bouncing off of trees and brush. His eyes wandered for a moment to catch the glimmer of two white lights blinking in and out a few yards away. With his head cocked to one side, he noticed a pair elsewhere doing the same.

His pace slowed as he looked about in every direction. There were dozens of little white lights blinking about. At once, he recognized the reflection of what must have been hundreds of tiny spiders along the ground and tops of saw palmetto, all staring at the father and son, reflecting the light of Marvin's headlamp as they passed by.

But now the little lights were growing dimmer. Leland hadn't yet realized that he came to a stop while looking at the glowing eyes. The lights blinked out one last time. Leland shot his head forward. His father was gone. The light was only a spark, one last moment of flashing around the shadows of trees and leaves before invisible.

His heart stopped. He couldn't hear his father's footsteps any longer. He could only hear the sound of crickets and alate termites flying around him. He was standing in complete darkness. He had no idea what to do as he fumbled around his pockets and clothes, looking for anything that may help him. Eventually, he mustered the courage to take a step forward, hoping not to trip on the uneven ground.

CRUNCH!

What was that?! The sound of a large footstep on top of the brush, not too far away from him. He would not take another step, too scared to make any noise, terrified to move.

The sound came again, a large crunch of leaves and branches rubbing against some large animal, out there, covered in darkness, and yet somehow all around him. His heart began to race. He could hear the blood coursing through his veins. He thought he might vomit.

"Papa!" Leland cried out as he started running forward into the darkness, the direction of where he hoped the light was last present.

He stumbled across the terrain, scraping his knees and shins as he fought through brambles and thickets in the darkness. He was positive that he was being chased by some predator, yet unable to identify if all that sound he was hearing was being made by the forest, or just himself.

He cried out again, "Papa, where are you?!" Just then, he tripped over a cypress knee and fell to the ground, his face bleeding, his ears ringing, and his nose numb.

I oftentimes ride my bicycle to work. It's only a 2.8-mile journey from my house to the church and takes me about thirteen minutes to get there, depending on traffic. The ride can be absolutely dreadful in the Florida summer sun, heat index reaching two billion degrees. But I find it relaxing and motivating for the day.

I have a bag attached to the back of my bike, with essentials in it, including a change of clothes for the day, a bottle of shampoo, hair product, Allen Wrenches and screwdriver. I'm decked out for safety with a little rear-view mirror on my helmet and lights all over my bike at the front and rear, with colorful strobes around the spokes of my tires. I have my obligatory water bottle and bike lock, as well as a little mini Bluetooth speaker to keep me motivated with *Martin Smith's* angelic voice. I may look a little ridiculous at times, carrying so much equipment on my hybrid, but I've always enjoyed gadgets, and would happily stick five more pounds of stuff onboard if I deemed it cool enough.

There is about a half-mile of my northbound ride that gets a little hairy. The road thins, but the traffic remains heavy, cars zooming past. There are three types of drivers that pass cyclists on the road. The majority seem to have some concept of passing by someone and understand their depth of field. They are the first type.

The second type are the slow and terrified. They creep up right behind your back tire and refuse to allow themselves to pass until all oncoming traffic has dispersed when they purpose that the only way to pass a two-foot-wide individual is to cross ten feet away from them into the other lane. They always race to do this as well, to make up for the time they lost, unnecessarily waiting next to you. Honestly, this seemingly terrified and unstable individual isn't the most calming presence when they are next to your vulnerable skin on the road, but they are nothing compared to the third type.

The third type of driver I can't give the proper label to, because I expect some children to read this book. They are the ones who seemingly have no concept of others on the road. You've met these people before. They blare their music and fail to look at their blind spots while touching up their makeup and checking their email. Now imagine being on a bike as they race by you within inches. They are the confident and bold. The reckless and obtuse. And honestly, I tend to drive like them occasionally when in my truck.

When I'm riding on that little strip of a half-mile, I am intently focused on my riding ability more than usual, in the occurrence that one of the latter two may show up next to me at any moment. I stare at the line on the edge of the road, just below my tire, as my father taught me:

> *"How do you ride on the very edge of the road like that?" I asked, as my little mountain bike continued to waiver in and out of the grass and asphalt.*
>
> *My father yelled back. "Because I'm not looking at the grass." He turned his bike in a large arc, circling around behind me. "I'm looking at where I'm going."*
>
> *He rode up next to me. "You go where your eyes lead. If you are too worried about the grass off to the side, you will only veer off in that direction. Stare at the white line, and you will ride straight."*
>
> *I looked down at the road, furrowed brow, frustratedly trying to stay on that three-inch-wide white line. My tire started wobbling again. I glanced off to the side to avoid the grass, immediately dipping into someone's yard again. My father chuckled under his breath and rode past me. "You'll get it."*

"Lord! If it is You, command me to come to You." Peter eagerly stared from the edge of the boat, squinting his eyes in the falling rain, leaning out into the misty night. "…Out on the water."[14]

Jesus was only a foggy silhouette, diluted by the crashing waves and lightning strikes. The wind howled around the boat, forming clouds around the fisherman.

The other disciples looked at one another and Peter. "Peter, what are you doing?!" James asked him.

"Come." Jesus' voice pierced through the darkness. Lightning cracked, briefly filling the sky with light and showing His smiling face.

Peter started to climb out of the boat, his eyes fixed on the figure in the darkness. "Peter," James said, trying to grab at him. "This isn't funny. Get back—" He stopped as he looked in disbelief. Peter was standing on the water.

A wave came and smacked Peter directly in the face, but did not phase him, as he turned toward Jesus with a stupid grin of joy. He walked toward Jesus' silhouette in the darkness. Jesus continued walking to meet him.

As he took a few more steps, Peter looked at the surrounding waves. He glanced back at the boat and realized he was over ten feet from it now. Another wave came and splashed him again. The rain poured down. The wind howled and deafened his ears. Lightning struck the heavens, and the thunder roared down.

He looked at his feet and saw they were beginning to sink below the surface of the water. His heart pounding, he started to run toward Jesus. But his feet would not move through the slush and waves. They began to sink quicker, and before he could realize what was happening, he was already up to his torso in water. He cried out, "Lord, save me!" just as the water filled his mouth, covered his head, and left his hand sticking out of the water.

The next moment Peter was standing again, doubled over and coughing the water out of his lungs. Jesus was patting him on his back as he recovered. Peter looked up at him, red-eyed and exhausted. Jesus smiled and shook his head. He laughed to himself, "Oh, Peter. Why did you doubt that I wouldn't be here to catch you?"

The two men walked back toward the boat, the waves and storm continuing to crash around them. As they approached the bow, the other disciples were staring, mouths agape and in disbelief. "Truly, truly you are the Son of God," they said.

Our faith measures only by our unwillingness to question God due to circumstance. Nothing compares to God. Fear is borne from the idea that God is not all-powerful, always loving and always with us. If we draw our eyes from our Father, or we look away from the path before us, we will find ourselves lost, crashed, and sinking.

My grandfather looked away from Marvin because of distraction. I looked away from the bike path because of fear. Peter looked away from Jesus because of both. If the Enemy, the weak sniveling pest that he is, can get you distracted from your calling, or fearful of the night, you will become hesitant to trust God, thus rendered ineffectual.

Of course, God is in the night! He stands amidst the waves, calling you deeper—deeper into your faith, your purpose, and most of all, your trust in Him. Keep your eyes straight. Do not take them off of the Father. Listen through the storm and know He is on the other side of the wave.

Your failure is not your destiny. Ironically, failure is a necessity for the acquisition of it. Too many of us believe that our failures end our greatness, when in fact they initiate, catalyze and define it. I did not become better at riding the day my father taught me about my focus. But I did become a better rider because I both understood my weakness and the solution to resolve it.

Peter did not walk on the waves perfectly. But he *did* walk on the waves! His failure—and subsequent rescue—was the thing that would remind him many months later that Jesus would always be there to catch him, even if he denied his love of Jesus publicly to a little girl.[15]

When my grandfather Leland was a teenager, he would go hunting with his father during hot summer droughts. The Everglades would dry up and leave nothing but brush and dead trees. The reptiles would curl up wherever they could to stay out of the heat, leaving rattlesnakes and copperheads all over the deer-paths. Leland would fearfully follow so close to his father that Marvin would nearly trip over him. But Marvin didn't care about the snakes at all. He would trample through the paths, kicking brush and bramble as he went, making himself appear to be as big as an elephant. This sent the rattlers and moccasins skirting out of the way as fast as they could; he never hesitated to send one flying with his boot either.

As Leland knew and understood, he didn't have to run away from the forest, he only had to run to his father's side; his father was bigger than anything the forest had to throw at him. His father was fearless. And though life will certainly throw terrible things at you, you aren't meant to run, tail between your legs, for the exit. You are meant to get as close to your Father as you possibly can and keep going. Faith doesn't deny a problem's existence; it only denies its influence. Stop letting a problem influence what you are willing to believe for, and just believe.

It's not a question of *if* you were made for greatness. It's a question of when you will stop being selfish and afraid and start being great.

PART 3:
Legend Character

*"The only thing that walks back from the tomb with the mourners
and refuses to be buried is the character of a man.
This is true. What a man is survives him. It can never be buried."*

- J. R. Miller

i. what is in our bones

When I think of dreamers and, more importantly, those that have accomplished their dream, my thoughts cannot wander long without inevitably arriving at Abraham. He is, to me, the principal believer of God's promises. While I'm sure it could be argued that other great men and women in God's Word were more so, perhaps Paul, David, or Esther; nevertheless, I have a deep resonating connection to Abraham's heart. He was a man that believed and waited for God to fulfill His promises for decades, faced with impossibility. I am challenged by his patience and belief that God would do what He had promised. And while his faith was not *perfect*, it was everlasting. Even after having received the gift, Abraham was willing to sacrifice all of it at the top of a mountain in Moriah.[1]

We do not see every bit of Abraham's life, such as anyone else in the Word of God, more often only the cliff-notes of faith and historical moments. Nonetheless, the experience of waiting for that set amount of time changed him from a man of earth to a man of faith. And therein lies why God gives us dreams deep in our hearts at such an early stage; why we sometimes find ourselves dreaming to do things that are impossible.

Truly, it is because God loves to accomplish the impossible. When one says, "it is impossible", and another stands in faith is the moment when He most often shows up. What better way to make sure no one else gets the credit!

But I believe there is a second byproduct of His dream in your heart. I believe your dream is the bait God has set for you. He absolutely does not care about what *you* will accomplish *upon this earth* near as much as what *He* will accomplish *in you*. What looks like your dream is the snare God uses to turn you into the man or woman He desires you to be. Therefore, it is impossible for you to accomplish your dream, to the fullest of God's willingness and grace, without first *becoming* the son or daughter God desires you to be.

Now, of course, not one of us will fully arrive at perfection, this side of heaven, but we must walk and work out our salvation on a continual trembling basis if we are to take steps toward our dream. And in truth, the dream you have now is not big enough yet, just as your character is not big enough to contain it. No eye has seen, nor ear heard, nor heart dreamed the depths of what God the Father has in store for those that love Him.[2] As your character grows, you will see God fulfill more of your dream. And as He fulfills your dream, you will see more ahead of you. The achievement of many and more dreams set men and women apart from those that came before them.

But we cannot obtain it without the container of character. You must work on *you* before you work on the dream. Your relationships, integrity, honor, pride, anger, emotions, lust, and ability to learn are the defining marks of true character.

Every person on God's green earth responds to circumstance in different ways. We were all created equal, but ultimately unique in our personality, understanding, intuition and ability. While we may be very different, most every one of our responses to failure or frustration boil down to three unique emotions: Anger, Fear, and Shame.

Imagine for a moment; you are amid a group of your colleagues. Not people particularly of the same personality or interest group, but all of you are directly connected, let's say, via coworker or church member. And all of you at the same moment hear the news of a fatal car accident the night before last, involving your shared friend's father. Some in the group would immediately get enraged; spouting off about how it is the fault of reckless drivers, poor car manufacturing, or the devil. Others would become introspective and fearful, perhaps leaving the conversation, and afterward texting and calling loved ones to make sure they are safe and using their seatbelts properly, never exceeding the speed limit. Finally, a third group would become sorrowful and ashamed; *how* could they ever have let Susie's father die, without first telling him how much he meant to them?

Every human personality revolves "around a powerful, largely unconscious emotional response to the loss of contact with the core of the self..."[3] When you experience failure or frustration, you will naturally respond with an emotion of anger, fear or shame. These three emotions are the core negative responses found inside of all people.

It's in our emotions, and our ability to wield and direct them, that determine our ability to succeed or fail in greatness or insignificance. Because it is in us, the three-part beings made of spirit, soul and body, that we find our internal struggle always pulling and prodding us in certain directions of thought, belief and action. Our body is mindless and obedient, only caring of its natural necessity, and easily swayed one way or the other. Our spirit is holy, perfectly aligned and enriched by God's. But it is our soul, the container of our thoughts, desires and emotions, that pushes one way or the other; toward God or toward selfishness.

While great thinkers and leaders have said it is dangerous to *follow* your emotions, it's doubly important to proactively learn to *lead* your emotions. Pity, the great consensus today is filled with malnourishing victual as "just do you" and "your feelings define you". What lies! Our feelings don't define us; how we control them defines us.

If we can strengthen and bolster our character, most importantly the emotions that drive our decision making, amidst failure and frustration, we can truly turn the tide in our hearts toward anything. It is a face-off with our *anger*, *fear*, and *shame*.

ii. on anger

"Their rage supplies them with weapons."
> *- Virgil*

Alderman men historically have bad tempers. I don't know what it is, but it has always run in our family. As a child, I would bottle down frustration and anger until it burst out in a storm of rage, sometimes resulting in my sister and me punching and kicking each other in the faces.

I recall a time I was only fifteen-years-old, climbing a tree with a new friend at his house when he thought it would be funny to step on my hands while I was trying to release and fall to the ground. I started to panic; hurt and fearful I may fall awkwardly. Looking up, I saw him cackling above and acting as if he would spit right into my face. He thought better of it when he saw my eyes. We hadn't been friends for very long, but I gave him the sort of stare that made him understand if he didn't remove his feet from my hands at that moment, I would beat the living daylights out of him.

In fact, it was much worse than that. He let off my hands, scurrying up the tree away from me, as I cooled down at the base of the tree. I had so much rage and anger inside me; I could feel a rooted desire to kill him at that moment. Of course, my logic was still in the back of my mind, telling me to sit and calm down, but I had an animalistic rage coursing through my veins that took a long time to subside. Regardless, it was a good thing he went up the tree for about fifteen minutes to give me space.

When my father was a brand new father, and my oldest sister Rachel was only six-months-old, he too had a similar sobering moment. Being a parent is no easy task, and I believe without God's grace and wisdom, it is impossible to do it successfully. Even with those, our human nature can rear its ugly face out like a possessed meerkat on the prairie. One such moment, my father was so frustrated, tired, and fed up with life, he found himself taking his frustration out on crying and hysterical baby Rachel, throwing her down on the bed.

The moment he did, it scared him to death. Not because he hurt her, which he hadn't, but because he knew the thing that caused it was out of his control. It was rage and anger, and it was without reason; the same kind of rage he had experienced from his father and grandfather while growing up.

When growing up, my great-grandfather Marvin and his brother Clarence were hot-tempered as well, but in different ways. Clarence was much more ornery and vocally assaulted Marvin on frequent occasions about anything he could think of. That Marvin was small and a pretty-boy was an oft-used point of conflict.

Once, while the two of them were still young boys, they wrestled outside the house, as their father Doll grilled dinner nearby. Clarence was picking on Marvin that evening, having the time of his life annoying his smaller brother. Marvin was quiet, but seething inside. Finally, fed up with Clarence's constant berating, he grabbed a grill poker from beside his father, and before Clarence could realize what was happening, he had thrown it at Clarence as hard as possible. It lodged itself in the back of his calf, sticking straight out.

Clarence did not stand to look at it or mend his wound. Instead, he ran as fast as he could into a field away from Marvin in hot pursuit. He knew that if Marvin caught him, he would have killed him. The leg could wait.

Underneath the raw and foolhardy approaches to anger, are the supernatural attributes that God breathed into us. While anger leading to rage can murder and assault, anger leading to passion can be holy.

There are only a few moments in Jesus' ministry where each Gospel writer records the same instance, as each man of God was impacted differently, thus expressed the ministry of Jesus in slightly different ways. Matthew, Mark and John were all impacted by Jesus' flushing of the temple marketplace, though.

During that time, all who entered the temple were required to bring their offering and sacrifice, in order that they may set things right with God and live purely before the King of the Universe. However, the world was corrupt; most of the rich were only rich because they made wealth off the backs of the poor; the laymen didn't have the land or means to raise a lamb, or even a dove, to bring to God.

When the poor would come to the temple to worship, the priests stopped them because they hadn't a proper offering to sacrifice. Of course, the money-changers set up shop inside and outside the temple, making an easy wage off of the people's need for righteousness.

When the disciples and Jesus approached the temple in Jerusalem, the disciples saw their leader and Messiah burdened and enraged by the temple *selling salvation*. It has always been God's heart that His people should be near Him. And now a rule, outlandishly out of proportion, was keeping the meekest and weakest from being near Him most of all. And the temple was making money off of it, instead of preventing it.

I love the images of Jesus smiling, holding children, walking on the countryside and always in pure white robes. But I know that this is not a full picture of who Jesus was and what He looked like. No, he was a man that worked with his hands, built instruments out of wood and fished for his food. He walked for miles in the dirt every day, surrounded by thousands of people. He sweat. He smelled. He bled. And from this story alone, we know He could get furious.

I have been enraged in my life, but I don't know if I have ever been so mad that I immediately made a whip out of many ropes, and began whipping people until they left my presence. But Jesus has.

iii. on righteous anger

"There is no passion to be found playing small—
in settling for a life that is less
than the one you are capable of living."
- Nelson Mandela

A few years ago, I was serving as the worship leader under my good friend Bryan Moore's leadership as he pastored our youth ministry. During this season, I was studying under Bryan as closely as possible. I believed, and still do, that if you have a dream you are

71

trying to achieve, the quickest and most deliberate way to it is to help someone else succeed at their own, especially if it requires you to lay yours down, in order to help them achieve theirs.

Therefore, I not only served him as his worship leader but in any way possible, hoping to glean as much as I possibly could from his tutelage. For years, I planted myself in his office every Wednesday morning, sometimes for hours, with nothing in particular to discuss. Sometimes, we had deep thought-provoking conversations, but oftentimes we only spent time with one another, and I cherished those moments of learning who this man was, inside-out. Of course, I also worked for him, whether in our graphics or production department and in youth ministry.

The thing about youth ministry is that the congregation is constantly evolving and changing. It ebbs and flows, determined by the time of the year, the average age of the students, and cultural surroundings. Some change can be anticipated and predicted, but often enough it is seemingly random.

During the fall, our youth ministry became highly influenced by a sense of dishonor and disrespect and lacked any great sense of maturity whatsoever. Not to say that I, or any of our leadership, resented students; we loved them and we were more than up for the challenge of leading, teaching and pastoring them. However, we found ourselves bogged by *correction* rather than edification, more often than not.

One night, Bryan was preaching on what the righteous anger of God looked like; what got *Him* fired up. Small pockets of students, scattered all about the room, were muttering and murmuring little jokes amongst themselves; it wasn't atypical.

Bryan continued teaching on honor and dishonor, and at this point in his message, he asked every leader present to stand, in order that we may properly honor them. Currently, our youth ministry had somewhere about twenty-five adults serving regularly; Bryan's heart was always that youth ministry wasn't possible without each of them consistently showing the students an example of love and direction. He prided us; he loved us.

I stood on the front row, next to Carlia and Bryan's wife Emily. But as the other leaders began to stand, little bursts of mocking claps and laughter erupted about the room; many students were openly deriding our leaders.

I looked over my shoulder and saw a few students leaning back in their seats and jeering. A leader was on her way to rebuke the group. Bryan kept on preaching, doing his best to not bring focus to the little attention-seekers. My gaze continued around the room and I caught the eyes of a young lady, whom I thought was one of our leaders I had yet to meet, for she was standing with the rest of us.

The girl's face was stoic and strong, so much so that she deceived me for a moment into believing she was, in fact, an adult leader. But the jig was up when she looked down at her friends next to her and broke into a silly smile, before sitting down. She thought twice about her decision to sit and stood again to sneer at the rest of the leaders' authority.

My stomach turned. The amount of disrespect to our leaders was unbearable in my bones. Not a disrespect that I felt for myself, for I couldn't care less what they thought of me at that point; but a disrespect for these leaders that I too loved greatly. They were my friends and confidants, that believed in the next generation with so much passion and determination, that they would consistently come each week and love each and every one of them, some for nearly a decade.

My blood boiled and my anger came bursting out before I could contain it. I walked over to the front of the sanctuary, between the stage and seats, Bryan standing behind me. I started yelling at the whole lot of the 120 students, though my attention and message were only for about ten of them, my voice projecting louder and louder over the heads of the students.

"I'm sick of this!" I screamed at the top of my lungs, my voice cracking under the weight of my adrenaline. "Sit your butts down and be quiet *now!*" A bit of honest applause started to trickle out of the surrounding students from those who were also irritated by the lack of respect in the room.

"No one applaud," I continued, "because I'm not done, and I'm pissed!" The group quickly shut up, and many faces stared at me, terrified.

"Do you see this man—" I pointed behind my back toward Bryan. "This man loves you more than anyone! I sit and serve with this man every week, and this man gives everything to love you. Everything to *serve* you. He believes in his whole heart that he can give you a better future than the crappy one you are on the way to! Do you think anyone loves you as much as this man, and what he gives every week for you?"

I continued on in a borderline manic demeanor as I described how the world as a whole thinks little of the teenage generation, and any role model in it of the artist, celebrity or athlete persuasion could never compare to what Bryan and our group of youth leaders brought them.

My whole outburst and wild screaming rebuke lasted a probable two minutes, but it shifted the environment of the entire night and weeks to come. I went back to my seat, sat down, a red hot raging mess full of emotion and adrenaline. I heard Emily whisper to Carlia, "That was *awesome.*"

Bryan actually thanked me as I sat down. I was so surprised how quiet and calm he was standing behind me during my escapade. He continued on with his message, "...as I was saying...God's *righteous anger—*"

That was one of the defining moments in my life that I learned my anger was not a disease. In my childhood, I was often ashamed of it. I tried to ignore or deny it. But as I grew older, and people would call me mean or demanding, I would grow irritated that they didn't understand what I was angry at. I'm usually not angry at people, near as much as I am angry at the problem people create or find themselves in. And furthermore, I'm not really mad at the problem people create, but the lie that the Enemy deceives them with.

I was never mad at the students; I was mad that my friend and pastor was being so ridiculed; I was mad that a group of students was being hindered from learning the biblical lesson he was trying to teach them because others were disrupting the room. And finally, I was the angriest because a group of students was being tricked by the devil himself into thinking it was better to make a joke than to learn from this great man of God on stage.

I was never being *mean*, at least not in my mind. Instead, I was being passionate. And passion is a dangerous but ultimately powerful force to be driven by. If you can learn to direct your anger, instead of being led by it, you will know how to use it for great and mighty things. An added bonus: the kids I screamed at eventually got further connected and gave their lives to Christ the next summer.

iv. on passion's purpose

*"He who reigns within himself
and rules passions, desires, and fears
is more than a king."*
- *John Milton*

A few Christmas's ago, when AnnaBelle was four years old, she helped me bring the groceries to the front door. We stopped at the entry, and I put down my bags to rummage through my pocket for the key.

I looked at my sweet little 4-year-old, holding her small bag of groceries, doing her best to help me. I was so proud. Smiling, I asked, "AnnaBelle, will you change the world with me?"

It was night; our house was lit by twinkling Christmas lights. The blinking colors above us cast a red shadow across her face as she looked down, forlornly. "I *want* to dad…" She whispered. "But how do we do it?"

My chest swelled with pride. I knelt down in front of her, putting my hands on her shoulders and lowering my head to meet her eyeline. "—By loving God and loving His people."

What moves my heart is knowing that AnnaBelle's desire outweighed her natural ability. Never have I, as a father, been disappointed by the idea that my children would try harder and dream bigger than what they were currently capable of. And neither has God the Father regretted you dreaming in the same manner.

Our lack of knowledge or understanding is always secondary to our *want and desire*. Our ability cannot determine our dreams. Rather, our dreams must motivate the acquisition of our abilities. With God, *nothing* is impossible.[4] Therefore, our dreams must not be hindered by the impossible. No matter what, the *"want to"* is more important than the *"how to"*. In this, you will find yourself led by passion.

In today's culture, we define passion as *a strong and barely controllable emotion.*[5] It is an intense desire or enthusiasm for something. But at its root, passion comes from the Greek word *paschō* which means *"to be affected or have been affected; to feel; to undergo; in a good sense, to be well off; in a bad sense, to suffer sadly."*[6]

It is neither positive nor negative; it is neutral. The intense emotional reciprocation to something intense having occurred. Therefore, in Acts 1:3, Jesus' death and suffering are described as quite literally His *"passion"*.[7] But His passion is to become *our passion*. Paul encourages the Church of Corinth that even when we, as Christians, are weighed down with troubles, it is for others to receive comfort and salvation. This is the motivation to patiently endure what we *suffer* or to endure *our passion.*[8]

Our "trials and tribulations" are not meant to be our "suffering and pain". They are meant to be our *motivation*; the call of what we are supposed to be and supposed to do. We are meant to turn pain and suffering into our motivation and passion for changing the world. And even when they weigh us down, it is for the world's comfort and salvation.

Don't hide from your pain. Use it.

Don't hide from your anger. Direct it.

And that is the purpose of pain leading to passion. When we fall down and cut our knees on what we have seen, experienced, or fallen victim, we use it to light the fire inside of us, that propels us to change the world. The pain which the Enemy brought to defeat us becomes the thing we use to destroy him.

Suffering is part of our lives on earth, and anger is put in us from God. But we were not meant to be stopped by our suffering, and we were not meant to let our anger destroy us with rage. We are supposed to eat our suffering and turn it into something beautiful.

Every lie that was told to us, and every time we were picked on; each moment we were harassed, abandoned, abused, molested or hurt are the moments that motivate our passion into letting no one else face that atrocity.

God *is passion*; He was, and still is, willing to give *everything*. Like Abraham, He gave His one and only Son. He directed His anger at His Son, to set us free in Christ Jesus.[9] Jesus directed his anger at the liar who sold salvation for a price.[10] And we must direct our anger toward answering the question of people's purpose and canceling the lie that they have none. Redirect your anger and use your pain to be the fire inside of your destiny and legend.

When I was born, I was minutes away from losing consciousness and experiencing permanent brain damage due to a nuchal cord. At age ten, I almost drowned in the ocean. At age 16, I was in an automobile collision that sent my vehicle flying into a wood, and I had every part of my face cut open by the force of the impact. My first child experienced arrhythmia while still in utero, and nearly removed weeks before her full term, putting her and my wife's life at risk. My third child died at seven weeks old due to presumably three different diseases and rose from the dead by the power of prayer.

Of course, pain has been in my life. But I have chosen to use every amount to fight what the enemy has tried *and failed* to stop me from doing. Your story looks different from mine, in every way. You can name many pains, failures and disappointments in your life, some worse and some less than my own. You can recall abandonment and betrayal that hurt your heart just thinking of them.

But God has designed you to take that hurt and create power. If you will call upon the name of the Lord in your pain, He will be there with you.[11] Your pain coupled with His promise creates power in your passion.

Use your pain to slap the devil that brought it in the face. It may not mean you don't experience pain ever again, but you will gain strength and boldness in the process.[12] Our greatest heroes and leaders were products of pain that they learned to overcome with God's grace.[13]

v. on fear

"When I was learning to creep,
my mother set me down on the beach to see what I thought of it.
I crawled straight for the coming wave
and was just through the wall of green when she caught my heels."
- Sylvia Plath

Around 430 years before Christ was born, God's people were conquered and in disarray. Jerusalem's walls had been torn down, and the Babylonian army tortured and molested the Jews for decades. For 70 years, God's people had nowhere to call home and nowhere to worship their God.

Nehemiah[14], a Jew, knew of the problem, and acting as cupbearer of the Persian King Artaxerxes, he was granted permission to return to Jerusalem, in order to rebuild the wall and protect Jerusalem again. However, upon his arrival, Nehemiah was stopped by those who oversaw and persecuted the city of Jerusalem on a daily basis. With only a few men, Nehemiah snuck into Jerusalem in the dead of night and rallied God's people to join him in rebuilding the wall.

The Jews were horrified and at wit's end. Every day, they suffered potential theft, murder or rape. They had to sell their children into slavery and give away their daughters, just to make ends meet. But hope came and knocked on their door.

With Nehemiah leading them, the Jews started gathering every piece of scrap that they could find. All over the city of Jerusalem, different tribes heard the call and began working. And by the hand of God, it only took 52 days to repair the entire wall of Jerusalem, making it a city of safety and strength again for all of God's children. The wall shamed and frightened the enemy outside the gates, as they stood in disbelief of the power of God.

Six days later, over 42,000 of God's children gathered in safety, for the first moment in a lifetime. Ezra, the prophet, stood before all of them and read from the Book of the Law. To most of these men and women, it was the first time they had ever seen or heard it. They wept in joy and sorrow as Ezra read aloud.

When Ezra was finished, Nehemiah, the newly appointed governor and former cupbearer, stood before the people. "Don't mourn or weep on such a day as this!" He cried aloud for all of the city to hear. "Today is a sacred day before the Lord your God. Go and celebrate! Don't be dejected and sad, for the joy of the Lord is your strength!" And the people left that place and went and celebrated together, sharing meals, gifts and stories, because they had heard God's words and *understood* them.

Many decades before Nehemiah would utter these words of encouragement, the prophet Jeremiah[15] lamented at the fall of Jerusalem to the hands of the Babylonians. But his sorrowful words had reminders of hope throughout them. He declared that God's faithful love would never end and His mercies would begin afresh each morning. Jeremiah looked upon the landscape of destruction and knew God would right the path.

One man saw the beginning of the hell and reminded his people not to be afraid—but that God would bring a new morning. Another man saw the end of the hell and reminded his people not to be afraid—that God's joy was found in being our strength. God is the same, yesterday, today and tomorrow[16]. He will always bring newness,[17] fight for us,[18] and enjoy doing it.[19] No matter our circumstance, whether walking *into* or *out of* tribulation, we must remember He is the same, and He is for us.[20]

When fear comes, *and it will*, God remains the same.

For our eight-year anniversary, Carlia and I celebrated in Quintana Roo, Mexico. We spent a few days shopping in Playa del Carmen, relaxing on the beaches of Akumal, and eating in the canopy of Tulum. One day we spent deep in the jungle at the Cenote Dos Ojos.

A cenote is an underground cave in which the ceiling has collapsed due to limestone erosion. The water is rich in mineral, and like a spring, stays a constant temperature all year round. It's an experience similar to a swimming-pool found in a cave.

The drag out to the cenote was right off the main highway. However, the road itself was little more than a single lane dirt road, eroded away by rain so badly we had one tire off the road at all times. Don't tell the car rental but that little Volkswagen went through a lot of pain on the mile drive out to the cenote.

What made matters worse was that our ticket to get into the cenote needed to be purchased along the highway, before we ever started the drive down toward Dos Ojos. We didn't know this until we had already driven to the entrance of Dos Ojos and were told to make the drive back. So we officially made the drive four times, up and down, covering our Golf in sediment from head to tire.

When we finally were inside the Dos Ojos gated development, the beauty of the natural landscape didn't disappoint. The cenote itself took our breath away. We walked down a long wooden stairway onto a gravel path that weaved through Quenepa and Ceiba trees, approaching the mouth of the cave.

The cave was enormous. Before we even began swimming, I put my face in the water with a pair of goggles and saw divers disappearing behind a cavern wall, some 30 feet below us. The mouth of the cave circled around the piece of land we sat on for a few hundred feet; the water sneaking under different tunnels and through rocky caverns, finding openings all over the land for miles.

The water's edge glittered in our eyes as we sat on a wooden dock, putting our flippers and snorkels on, securing our flashlights around our necks. We gently fell into the refreshing water and immediately felt little fish nibbling on our toes and fingertips. One such fish followed me around incessantly, chewing on my back and utterly antagonizing me for the entire day.

Regardless of my fish nemesis, the whole experience was breath-taking. Stalactites reached down from above us like spindly hands trying to rip the goggles from our faces, while stalagmites powerfully shouldered their way up from the depths, standing like tree trunks in our way as we swam around them.

While I absolutely delighted myself, Carlia was having a rather hard go at all of it. She isn't the strongest swimmer, and even less confident with snorkeling. The cold water gave her a chill, and not too long after being in the water, she just as rather sit on the edge and take photos of the whole experience.

Once she left me, I ventured out to the edge of the cave and crept along, testing the depths and my breath-holding. I was easily floating at 40-foot depths. Paddling along the placid water, I finally came upon a little wooden sign next to some copper piping running along with the ceiling of the cave. It was the kind of sign you expect to read "DANGER" in old western-styled nickelodeons. But the red paint, smeared from years of wear and tear, simply read two words: "*Bat Cave*".

My affinity for bats is unmatched. I find them very fascinating and beautiful creatures. It doesn't hurt that my favorite comic book hero has always been *the Batman*. But the bat itself is an extraordinary creature. The only mammal that flies, each bat can consume 1,000 insects in less than an hour, eating its entire body weight every night. The largest colony of bats in America eats over 250 tons of insects every night.

Bats can get up to speeds of over 60 mph, and the fastest was recently recorded at over 100 mph. They have often received a bad reputation of being monsters and bloodsuckers, even though only three of the 1,200 species of bat are vampiric, and they don't suck blood, they lap it up. I suppose their oddities, and subsequent notoriety, are some reasons I have grown fond of them in my life.

When I read *"Bat Cave"*, I felt like a kid in a candy store. Immediately, I ducked under the water, shining my light beyond the wall of the cavern. The light cut through the darkness like a knife, and the great beam shown on a pocket of air only a few feet ahead in the darkness. I came up for air again before diving under and propelling myself forward.

The next instant, one of the most ironic and surreal moments of my life occurred (to which there have been many). My flashlight began flickering. The reflection of the cave walls blinked on and off, disappearing from around me as my flashlight started to give up. Complete darkness enveloped me like two great hands slowly closing in. I scrambled under the water, looking at my flashlight, slapping the side of it, praying it would come back, all the while thinking to myself that I had somehow swum into a horror movie.

I thought better of myself to preserve what little battery there was and turned the flashlight off. I came up in the cave, completely surrounded by absolute darkness. I heard the sound of my breath and the water slowly splashing away. It's a very eerie feeling to not be able to see anything and hear only your heavy exhale.

I calmed down and let myself rest, telling myself that I was only a few feet from light and civilization. All I had to do was drop down and turn back six or seven feet. But then I heard the sound that would change everything.

Pseet Pseet...

I could hear them; the flutter of their wings and little voices peeping from out there in the darkness. They weren't next to me, but they were close. I turned my flashlight back on and to my delight, it came back fully. I slowly ventured forward in the water, bending around a wall, and to my amazement, discovered that I was actually in a very large cavern. Just ahead of me was a solid beam of light, coming through a cave hole in the ceiling above.

I swam toward the light, dropping underwater again to get my bearings. As I went under, I was astonished by how well-lit the water was from its skylight. I could easily see every edge of the cave, stretching out. Some 70 or 80 feet to my left, through many winding rock structures, I could see the dim light reflection of a few divers deep underwater.

Directly under the skylight was a large rock that I was able to creep up and rest upon. I took my mask off and looking up, I could see the jungle above. No matter what, I could always get out that way or with the help of the divers, albeit a very dramatic and awkward rest of my day.

Finally, I looked about at the cave ceiling. I could see dozens of little brown bats, nuzzled together in their upside perch. My light startled a few of them, even though it was dimly working again.

They dropped, air caught their wings, and they fluttered all around me. I listened to their quiet song and tried my best to take in every aspect of this moment. I presumed there would be few like it in my lifetime.

The truly awful thing was that with every moment spent enjoying myself, I had the terrible feeling that I was losing precious seconds of battery use in my flashlight. I was doing my best to experience this cave that God's hands built, all the while terrified by this nasty little voice in the back of my head that it would be my grave.

I spent about five minutes on the large rock, taking little mental pictures as best I could before I started to swim back from where I came. After about twenty feet of swimming, I realized it hadn't taken this long for me to approach the skylight rock the first time. I went underwater and nothing looked familiar. The ground was higher here, and smooth sand was beneath me. This was not the way I had come in.

Panic filled my veins with blood pumping through them. My heart rate quickened, even at the pleading of my head telling me to calm down, *"Calm down. Take a breath. Calm down."*

At least I had the rock under the skylight as a landmark. I swam back to it, watching my flashlight slowly flicker out again. I turned it off, now that I was under the light.

I came around the edge of the rock and looked back to where I first saw the divers. They were further away now, their lights starting to become shadows 100 feet from me. I took a breath, praying for God to give me clarity, and started swimming in the direction I thought best.

I swam for another twenty feet and panic started to rise in me again. *This was the wrong way too!* I was lost and had no idea how much longer my flashlight would hang on. It was barely usable at this point, only shining a few feet in front of me and sporadically blinking all the way out. Worse, the further I swam from the skylight, the darker everything became.

Then I recognized the back of the cave wall I first swam around. Relief settled into me as I finally knew where I was. As I ventured to the other side of it, the world become bleak, dark and small again. I made my way through the rock stalagmites, trying not to bruise my knees in the darkness. Each time I came up for air, I had to reach my hand above and push against the ceiling of the cave, preventing my head from bashing against it. The whole process didn't take very long but was grueling and unsettling.

I found the copper piping next to the *Bat Cave* sign, now on this side of the entrance. I briefly turned back to the cavern, saying one last goodbye to a dream come true and listening one last time to the chirp of my fluttering friends. I dove under the water, and just as I did, my flashlight blinked out for the last time.

I could see light ahead of me, daylight. I pumped my legs, ready to be free of the cave. I burst up on the other side of the cave wall. I was back.

In the distance, a diving instructor started yelling something at me in Spanish that I didn't quite understand. I realized he was shouting to ensure I had a flashlight with my intention to go that way.

I held up my flashlight to him, hollering back, *"Flashlight!* I got one!" My flashlight never turned on again. Worst $20 spent ever.

Our passions will lead us face to face with our fears. We can either swim through our fear, into our dreams or turn back. Our amount of courage, or cowardice, will determine the length and weight of our earthly purpose. God has not given us a spirit of fear, but one of power, love and a clear mind.

All fear is inherited by our failure or the fear given by those we trust. We are not born with fear; we acquire it. The fear of bats, snakes or spiders was only put in someone by the fear belonging to someone else, perhaps a parent or schoolmate. The failure and endured mockery, or perhaps even the lack of experience, has made many afraid to publicly speak.

Social media has shaped a generation into not fully knowing how to express themselves face to face with someone, and thus, has created a generation likely to be afraid of conflict, unaware of how to resolve it. While sarcasm and the fear of being left out have turned many bitter and spiteful, afraid that no one is truly authentic.

Fear is learnt—not natural. God never designed you to be afraid. He never even designed you to be cautious.[21] He only designed you to be wise, and when your wisdom tells you something is foolish or dangerous, you can avoid it. But not out of a fear of an arbitrary demise. You were designed to see the foolishness in sin and avoid it, therefore administering your wisdom and power, not your submission or weakness.

In 1960, psychologists Eleanor J. Gibson and R.D. Walk[22] studied the effects of depth perception in infants, intending to discover if it were a natural-born or acquired ability, brought on by age and development. In order to test this theory, the scientists created a special table for infant children to crawl upon. The table had a small wall along the sides to prevent the babies from crawling off the edge.

They made the floor of plexiglass, and underneath half of the large table was a checkerboard print. The other half appeared invisible due to the plexiglass, and on the actual floor, some four feet below was another checkerboard. This created the illusion that half the table were gone, and a visual cliff was at the half-way of the table. But of course, the infants were safe.

What Gibson and Walk discovered was that at certain ages, infants reacted differently to the visual cliff; some were afraid of it; others were confused. Babies who could not yet crawl didn't seem to have a fear of the cliff and would have fallen off had there been an actual drop.

Based upon their results, Gibson and Walk believed that children acquired the ability to perceive depths once they were able to crawl and move about in a three-dimensional space above differing heights. However, they also discovered that the *fear* of falling was not innately born into children either.

In fact, they postulated that it was trial and error, falling and tumbling, which a human encounters through life, that would then produce the *fear* of falling and tumbling. Those without a reason to fail would never believe it were even possible. This concluded that there may, in fact, be absolutely zero fears we as humans are born with, only those that we acquire through failure and pain or inherit through authority and shame.

What is truly remarkable about the *visual cliff experiment* is what they discovered when putting mothers in the room with the children. Children were always eager to race to their mother's arms when the mother would call them from the "safe" side. But when the mother called from the "cliff" side, the babies would not race toward her. However, that doesn't mean they would not come to her.

If the mother stood *frowning* on the cliff side, the infant would avoid it at all costs. If the mother stood *smiling* on the cliff side, meanwhile encouraging their child to crawl toward them, the baby at first may hesitate at the "cliff's edge", yet ultimately would venture out and race to his or her mother.

Some would roll right into the cliff, while others backed in slowly. It was apparent that while we may acquire fear, we have borne inside of us a trust factor, activated by our parent's beckoning, that if our parent calls to us and tells us it is safe, we will believe we can walk off a cliff.

Likely, something deep inside Peter told him he could walk on water, as long as his Father told him, smiling and confident, to come out upon it. You were designed to have no fear. And more importantly, you were designed to let go of any you acquired when your Father calls you. It seems our purpose if indeed found I our confidence, and confidence found in Christ (our faith).

You are not alone in fearing your death, and even more so in fearing your life won't actually amount to anything worth sharing. We all wonder if we will ever accomplish or finish anything important on earth before our eyes roll up and our bodies give in to time. And though this fear is prevalent, it can—and *should*—be a motivation to keep pumping your legs hard until you get to your dreams.

Where we trip up in our response to this fear is letting it stunt our growth. Fear acts as a catalyst to failure. Shaky hands are likely to veer the vehicle into the median. Likewise, shaky emotions are likely to veer a relationship into a divorce. Shaky decisions will veer businesses into the red. Your courage or cowardice will determine your reach.

And once more the fear extends beyond us, into the damnable belief that we may have missed our opportunity altogether, set upon by our cowardice responses to fear in our past. But take heart, for your purpose in life is not based upon the hundred years you have only on this planet.

Its small time on earth cannot weigh or sum the purpose of a soul. Instead, regardless of what one has accomplished or seen in this brief moment, it has a purpose and design made for eternity.

And that purpose, though it be affected by these moments, contains little that we know of, or *could* know about, this side of eternity.

This truth delivers two revelations that each person (dependent on their personality, age, and past) walks in and out of based on their emotional stability. One: (that most young people experience) is the frustration that we haven't even begun, and the things, conversations, and moments we think are most valuable, actually serve little to no consequence in the full picture. And two: (that those with more history, and thus, failures) is the relief that the things, conversations, and moments we are truly ashamed of, will actually serve little to no consequence in the full picture.

There is no doubt though, that every moment does indeed *matter*; each cause has an effect, and each action, both negative and positive, has a reaction. But the act of *fearing* such actions and reactions will only leave us more likely to create even *more* negative actions. Therefore, it is best to go about life fearing nothing at all, except maybe fear itself.

When fear strikes, swim harder; when the lights go out, keep going; when businesses fail, pick yourself up and try again; when relationships explode, learn from it and do better; when conflict arises, confront it; when prayers aren't answered, pray again; when bears get in your way, shoot them in the face until they fall down. And if we die trying, at least we die fighting.

vi. on fear's brother, shame

*"And they heard the sound of the Lord God walking in the garden
in the cool of the day, and Adam and his wife hid themselves
from the presence of the Lord God among the trees of the garden."*
- Genesis 3:8

When Sin came, it brought with it Shame. It caused the only two people on earth to fear the One they knew loved them more than anything; not because He was suddenly fearful, but because they feared they didn't deserve His love any longer. Shame's cycle is treacherous, and it will catch all of us in its snare at some point.

While many of us are better at hiding it, or seeming to forgive ourselves for our mistakes, every one of us knows that deep down, our sin has made us worthless. And that dangerous, ugly truth is used by the Spirit of Shame to push us down, just when we start to look up again.

For our intents and purposes, and because there are far too many sins to be shamed by, we will only discuss the obvious one that all have most likely faced. The sin of *lust* was not the original sin; however, it was an almost immediate byproduct of the greed and pride initiated by Adam and Eve.

Adam and Eve covered themselves with fig leaves after their sin; borne not from a perverted sexual desire between the two of them, nor based on a sudden environmental necessity; they were, after all, married and secluded, and had lived their entire lives comfortably outdoors. No, their desire to be covered came from a sickening feeling in their hearts; they felt vulnerable and unworthy. The same frightening feeling that makes a child pull the sheets over his or her face when they think a bogeyman is in the closet; they know deep down that the sheet changes nothing, but their vulnerability drives them into an irrational panic.

91

However, this lingering irrational fear of vulnerability had a long-term effect on the children of Adam and Eve. As a byproduct of covering one's vulnerability (which *has* been differing parts of the body over history, depending on the culture) you and I couldn't see a person in his or her entirety. And in this way, the perversion of lust was born. As stated, lust wasn't the origin of our sin‡, but it surely was a byproduct.

It is the same insipid desire for you and me to want to accelerate past the speed limit, as soon as we know what the limit is. I am perfectly fine driving at a speed of 65 mph. It is an adequate speed with great results. But as soon as the limit is 70 mph, something in me wants to go 78. *That* is sin at its root. The desire for more, when I have plenty. As Lewis said: "This itch to have things over again, as if life were a film that could be unrolled twice or even made to work backwards..."[23]

So what I couldn't see, and the manifestation of "not seeing", borne from the vulnerability and shame brought on by the nudity, created in me and mankind, a sexual desire and lust for more to witness. In a way, one could argue that *Law* created *Lust*. Though in reality, *shame* created it; because without the shame, there would be no law.

Whereas I'm sure we would be attracted to our spouses in paradise, the actual desire for one another's rear-ends and chests is only a byproduct of each of us having tried to physically cover our spiritual shame; as one covered more in guilt, another coveted in lust. *Where else would we get the desire for a rear-end?* It is merely a perversion of what should be a desire for the *entirety* of the spouse (spirit, soul and body) turned into a desire for only that which we can't immediately experience; proliferated by centuries of sin,

---

‡ that was *pride*, manifested by doubt in God's goodness.

shame, law and culture. This leads to the sole attraction being to that which I cannot see, and belittles and undervalues the rest of the three-part being. Often, I muse that if something suddenly snapped all of mankind into nudity—if not all awkwardness, shame and lust would dissipate in less than a fortnight.

In our western culture today, we are so confused by our own sexuality that we both embrace and are disgusted by it. At one moment, we celebrate people who express their sexuality to a fault, and the next moment we ridicule those that take it too far. Somehow, the woman who strips is celebrated for using the power of her body, while the man who watches is seen as a dog, taking advantage of her (though that is okay, because: "We are animals, after all" and "How else do you expect a man to act?"). Psychologically, the woman receives a counterfeit principle that her body—that *will deteriorate*—is her only asset and that men are weak-willed; meanwhile, the man slowly loses satisfaction with his own bride (or future bride) and ultimately feels inadequate at teaching his sons how to be men (because "he hasn't learned himself how to be a man —*the animal!*").

It would be best that the woman know her body is gold, but it is still only a third of the treasure that God made for her spouse one day. Her soul and spirit complete the full picture of her value. This is why men stay attracted to their brides after fifty, sixty and seventy years of marriage, because her body is only a *fraction* of her full beauty, and when it gradually changes with age, his love is founded on her heart and mind.

It would be best for the man to know that he was indeed made to be strong-willed, driven and passionate; that he is meant to get angry and wild, but his passion should be pointed at failure, brokenness, and sin. In a world that calls men *animals* for being wild, and encourages them emaciated and tender in every interaction, we have shoe-horned men to only be wild in the closet with their magazines and cell phones and tame in public. Men *should* be allowed angry and wild; they should just direct their anger and wildness at the thing (or more putting, the devil) that is causing their pain and the world's hurt.

Culture has twisted a view that pornography and nudity are expressionism and art. Corporations shout from the mountaintops that they believe in free will, all the while knowing their biggest marketing and equity comes from your addiction to sex—why else would they use sexual desire to sell you toothpaste? Meanwhile, human trafficking and the negative effects of the *Playboy* generations are thriving from it—directly influencing our view of people as objects of our amusement and pleasure; rather than the gods and goddesses they were designed to be.

And this continues on and on, into every area of how we look at ourselves and others. *Shame* drips from humanity like a disgusting old wound that will never heal. Each generation growing more ashamed of its nudity. I know grown men who change in the stall in the bathroom because they feel uncomfortable in the gym locker room.

Don't suppose that I am advocating we should all live like some nudist colony, with a blown-out-of-proportion idea that if we present ourselves like Adam and Eve, we will be closer to God. No, I am fully aware that I too have this same lust and perversion in me; because I have grown up under the same sun like you, with blatant onslaughts by advertisements, media and culture.

Yet, I do take the time to face the fear of my own personal shame and nudity. At the gym, I have found myself to be the only man under 50 who will strip down and change in the locker room, because this odd living in shame has happened to my generation and

I don't want to be afraid of what God originally intended, especially if it results in said shame.

We have been neutered by shame. And this, in turn, completes the cycle: more hiding creates more perversion, creates more sin, creates more fear, creates more shame, creates more hiding. If fear is the catalyst of sin and failure, its brother *shame* is the thing that sustains it; the nullifier of principle, because with *shame* comes hopelessness.

Carlia and I love the show *Lost*. We have binge-watched all the way through the series several times. It is six seasons of upending, never-ending twists, turns, questions and wow moments, that kept us trying to figure everything out during multiple viewings. But the reason we love it most of all is the development of such a rich cast of characters. *Lost* has one of the largest casts of any network television show, and almost every character was delicately drawn out for the viewer, learning and growing over the course of the show.

Two such characters are Jack and Sawyer. Jack is the steady leader who doesn't know how to lead himself. And Sawyer is the rascal conman who eventually learns to love. In the last season of the show,[24] without giving too much away (but let's face it, it's been off the air for over a decade; if I spoil it, it's your fault at this point), the group of islanders are facing off against a very dangerous kind of evil (let's call him Locke) that continues to trick and deceive each of the members in different ways.

Sawyer believes in Locke and thinks that Jack is wrong, *again*. He rashly undermines Jack and gets multiple crucial people killed in an ill-fated attempt to leave the island (they were in a submarine that exploded and sank).

When Sawyer, Jack and the last remaining survivors crawl themselves back onto shore, Sawyer looks out at the sea, despondently.

"I killed them," he says, turning to Jack, upon realizing his rebellion resulted in the loss of those who trusted him. "—didn't I?"

Jack boldly walks over to him, looking him in the eye. "*He* killed them," he says and walks away. Though Sawyer may have been the hands that did the deed, there was an evil force deceiving him into the fearful action. Jack knew that we do not fight against flesh and blood but against the power of darkness.

What's so interesting about *shame* is that we carry the weight of all our trouble on our shoulders and hide ourselves from anyone knowing; we try to do this especially to God. But at the end of the day, all of our sin, and all of our mistakes are thrown at us by one individual: the great sniveling little maggot known as Satan, who has made it his duty and privilege to torment, lie and deceive you from the moment you were born.

It's true that we were made worthless by our sin, but God has made us worthy by His Son. Shame is only shed when we purposefully take off the old dead skin and leave it behind, like Eustace "growing stronger and bigger"[25] in *The Voyage of the Dawn Treader*.

Complacency initiates sin. Fear Catalyzes it. Shame sustains it.

When King David lost his passion and purpose, he became complacent. And in doing so, he stayed at home, when he should have been on the frontline of his army. In his opulence, he slept with another man's wife Bathsheba, who in turn became pregnant. In his fearfulness, he murdered a good man Uriah, in an attempt to cover it up. And in his shame, he could not talk to God and achieve what he was meant to become.

In every way opposite, you were created to live and have purpose in your heart. Instead of complacency, you were made to live in passion; full of vision, drive, righteous anger and identity. Instead of fear, you were made to be brave; courageous in the face of failure and fear. Instead of shame, you were meant to live in confidence; fully assured of who you are, and most importantly, *whose* you are.

When we fully know and understand that we are God's children, we find ourselves more apt to walk out of sin, and even more so, *away* from sin. Shame has no hold on those that know God calls them son or daughter; it slides off like a Teflon coat.

Everyone sins; brought on by our complacency and lack of passion. Everyone has fear, in the respect that it comes to face us when failure occurs. But shame cannot stick to someone who is confidently walking with the Lord, and in *that*, it retroactively kills all sin in one's life. Confidence wipes away fear before it ever comes; courage creates purpose and passion inside of you. So in simple terms, if you know God loves you more than anything, you'll stop sinning.

You must have passion to become a legend; know that God put purpose in you.

You must face your fears to become a legend; know that God fights for you.

You must cancel your shame to become a legend; know that God loves you.

PART 4:
No One Can Steal Your Destiny

"It is not in the stars to hold our destiny,
but in ourselves."
- William Shakespeare

i. what comes before destruction

Marvin would let nothing shame him. Of course, that didn't necessarily mean that he had no shame. Every day, Marvin would wear a sharp, crisp white tee shirt under a suit and tie. The only time you would find him without a bowtie or bolo tie would be when he dressed down to hunt. He cared deeply about an immaculate, clean appearance. Of course, it didn't always rub other gruffer men the greatest way, when the pretty boy at only five foot six could get any girl.

One afternoon, on the side of a train junction, a group of men was heckling Marvin a "dandy"; they ridiculed him as weak and a momma's boy. Marvin's pride could not be undone, and foolishly he bargained them that he could carry a 100-pound bag of feed up and down a flight of twelve stairs, with only *his teeth*.

The men laughed and put their money on the figurative table at the side of the tracks. Sure enough, Marvin grabbed the bag of feed, hung it from the grip in his mouth, and began walking up the steps. Marvin was little, but he was a bull.

Up he went, and the men's mouths fell. On his way down, their deriding turned cheering, as this little man was doing what no man should be able. But Marvin's internal pride would be lost by his external weakness.

When he dropped the bag of feed at the men's feet and smiled in his success, his spine began to tickle and shake at the base of his back. Without warning, his legs came from under him and his back began to seize. He lay facedown in the dirt, screaming in agony. His backside uncontrollably began forcing its way up to his neck as his head reared backward, like his body were a crescent moon. His spine was snapping itself in half from the muscle's abuse.

It took three men to hold Marvin's legs, rear, back and neck in place for several minutes, until the muscles would relax and his back could return to its proper form. Marvin's pride nearly destroyed him in an instant; he was not unlike *Marty McFly* in that regard.

The irony of pride is that it is the close relative of shame, masked in self-denial of one's lack of ability or worth. Pride feeds shame, in a twisted view of *confidence*, that will only lead, whether through guilt, fear or loneliness, to a shame-filled depression and anxiety. But the sickening thing about pride is that it springs upon us at any moment§, even on our way out of depression and shame.

A confident Christian is only held up by the truth and understanding that their glory is present because of God's glory and presence. While the Enemy would love to distract you, terrify you

---

§ This is because our royalty is rooted deeply in our bones. Satan needs only to activate and twist the truth that our royalty comes from ourselves rather than God, and our humility will be dismembered.

or shame you with sin, he knows a bold individual is his greatest annoyance; however, it is not his greatest worry. If the Enemy can't distract you with simple sins or scare you with his arrows, he'll aim his attention at letting you destroy yourself with *pride*.

After seventeen years all over southern Florida, Marvin was pastoring the largest Church of God in Miami. He had started as a poor farmer, working cattle and orange groves to survive, and turned into one of the wealthiest men in southern Florida, using every bit of shrewdness, wheeling-and-dealing, and skills he had. He could hunt anywhere, build anything, and teach anyone. He had the prettiest wife in all of the South, and his oldest son Lewis was following in his footsteps, going to seminary at Lee Bible School (which would one day become Lee University) in Cleveland, Tennessee.

Lewis, however, was not the son that would create history as a minister, though he was absolutely called to preach and had a powerful presence. In 1946, a few months before graduation, a group of young men, including the school director's son, were caught vandalizing. Lewis himself was the look-out of the operation and received the most blame and punishment. He was kicked out of seminary, only a few days before graduation. The director's son was overlooked. No one knows what happened to the other boys.

Marvin was livid, not with Lewis, but the school. His invective was the Church "can't do that to *my* son!" He marched up to Tennessee and *took* Lewis away, rather than letting him get thrown out. And with that action, his hardness and refusal to be mocked or under-appreciated grew to an astonishing level. Marvin Alderman was powerful. He *was* the Church of God in Florida.

And so he quit.

Within only a few years, pride and shame roller-coastered through Marvin's soul. He stopped talking to God altogether; he began drinking; he could not forgive the men who had shamed him and therefore began sinning so defiantly that he never would be able to properly forgive himself. He cheated on his wife Mamie, sleeping around at different houses and with different women and wives in town, all the while losing his parsonage, resulting in his wife and four children no longer able to depend on him.

My granddaddy Leland would tell stories of living in a tar-paper shack, with only two rooms. There were no screens over the open windows, and at night palmetto bugs the size of field mice would fly through the room and terrorize him, as he cowered under a sheet on the couch. Later in his adult life, he could face his fear and kill the insects when needed, but he maliciously *hated* roaches for the rest of his life; the fear was always in him.

For the next several years, the Alderman's lived in poverty. Mamie would continue to raise the children, walking all of them to church every Sunday by herself, making Marvin drive them to Camp Meeting every summer, and working in a factory to provide for the family. But the family never had a dime, as anything she made was immediately spent in a bar by an inebriated Marvin angrily cursing and fighting invisible church leaders. His pride absolutely destroyed everything he had worked to accomplish and was destroying his family right before his eyes.

No one can steal your destiny. It is the thing laid out before you, and God is upon that path waiting to share and show you every step of the way. Great loss, pain and hurt are upon it. Great reward, joy and comfort also are riddled throughout that path. Most of all, that path has in it, a wild reward of purpose and true contentment. And no one can steal it from you, not one person or spirit. *Except you.*

What lies ahead of you can be delayed or destroyed by the actions of apathy, jealousy and pride. You will never get to your destination if you are unwilling to work tirelessly at everything set before you; you will delay your progress if you are in constant competition for your destiny; you will destroy all of it if you conclude that it was, or is, based on your merit.

God cannot promote you until you are ready to give something away. That's why we can't be afraid of change. Of course, change requires sacrifice, and sacrifice brings with it pain. It's that pain that makes good men and women afraid of becoming *great* men and women. The process of promotion begins with you relinquishing your present title, now; it means giving up what you like for what you need.

I have worked for my friend and Pastor Bryan Moore for nearly a decade now. And almost relentlessly, I have reminded him that I am coming after his job. I want to always be learning, growing and changing who I am, and I don't let him forget that he needs to give it all away to me.

At the same time, I work twice as hard to give every task I have away to those behind me. My title, position, or whatever nonsense I think I have acquired here on earth is nothing but a vapor. And if I stand in possession of it, I stand in the way of others reaching the goals God has set before them; therefore, I am not growing or going anywhere myself. After all, if I am standing, possessing a position, then I am not really moving.

It's better that you be a teacher twice as fast as you are a learner. Never stop learning, but doubly never stop teaching. What you teach, you retain, and what you duplicate, you empower. Therefore, you are exponentially more efficient. The positions we have on this earth would be greatly more effective if we would start giving them to those behind us and learning to steal the ones from those ahead of us. Of course, I use the term "stealing" rudely to describe the violent nature it requires of us if we are to become true *legends*. Jesus was always empowering his disciples to "go and feed them" and "go out and heal them". He refused to be the end-all-be-all of what God would do on the earth. He knew that it required the process of duplication and replication.

Life is a vapor,[1] and so is a title. It would be better to understand that a title, position, or rank is God's—not yours. This relieves you from both the stress of making sure you complete it to perfection (which is humanly impossible), and rescues you from the mistake of thinking anything good in your life is from your own power (which is humanly idiotic).

Furthermore, it saves you from the fear and constant obstacle of "making sure no one steals your future". How foolish we are to squabble and feel threatened when someone seemingly more talented, more special, more better-looking, more lingual, more charismatic, more wise, more, more, more, etc., comes along in our life—and we think we are going to lose everything we have worked hard for. God is our Father, creator, advocate, and boss. No one can steal your destiny; stop performing for man and perform only for God.

Bryan Moore and Pastor Dan Stallbaum sat with me in Bryan's office a few years ago to tell me that the pastoral team had concurred I was the right man to lead as youth pastor. I was ecstatic and overwhelmed; I hugged both of them. However, the turnover had to be a slow and delicate process; Bryan had been the youth pastor for over a decade, and some people may get upset or hurt in the announcement. I wasn't to discuss it with anyone save my wife and the pastoral staff for nearly six months.

Throughout the duration, I had a few strange conversations with different people in my office. Little comments would creep up like: "So are you the youth pastor of the whole church, or just this *one* campus?" and "So what exactly *is* your role?" For me it made sense that it would be the same as the pastor before me, especially when he and the senior pastor of the church were the two that spoke to me; but something was happening between the lines of these odd comments and the sighs and breaths of confusion intermingled throughout. In my head, I was hearing little voices of jealousy and frustration buried underneath my excitement and anticipation.

Furthermore, the feelings were escalated by the fact that I couldn't share the news with *anyone* for months; it began to feel like it would never happen or was somehow slipping away from me. What if they were changing their minds? What if someone else was better or more qualified? What if I had a naysayer, speaking negatively about me behind my back and making my pastors second guess their decision?

Comparing oneself to another, especially a believer to another brother or sister, is an endless waltz of frustration, and one that I had grown tired of many years before; it is a waste of sleepless nights and mind-numbing afternoons.

One such afternoon, while speaking with Bryan in my office about day-to-day tasks, I asked him bluntly what my role would be as the youth pastor. I've always appreciated our candid relationship. Though we may not always approach situations, in the same manner, we both trust enough to know we have one another's best interests in mind. Having those you can trust unconditionally in life is very important. I do not think just anyone can be this for an individual. In fact, I would argue that only one or two people *should* be this for you, and no one more.

Complete, unadulterated honesty with everyone will get you misunderstood, betrayed, hurt, and bitter more often than not. Of course, I'm not advocating that we openly *lie* to others; only that we understand and identify those that we can be frank with, those that we must explain in lengthier terms (and if we don't have the time for lengthier terms, then nothing at all), and those that would use knowledge to hurt us; therefore, not providing any ammo to them.

When I say unconditional trust and honesty, I mean just that. Though, I question if many have that sort of real relationship, save those that have been married for decades through thick and thin. True friendship and sacrifice are rare. Regardless, I have only a few people that I have *chosen* to be completely, yet imperfectly, authentic. And believe me, barring one's soul in utter dismay and truth is a very dangerous habit and absolutely a *choice*. This sort of thing doesn't happen naturally once you have grown up a little.

Bryan is one of those people, and consequently, he has experienced much of my belaboring frustration and outright tantrums over the years. When I asked him what my role would be as the youth pastor, he began telling me the same sort of bureaucratic jargon he expressed the first time. But I wouldn't let him, not because I didn't believe what he was saying, or that he himself didn't believe it, but because I needed to get to a brass tacks understanding or my head would explode from conjecture.

"Just tell me what *you* think—" I interrupted. "I understand what I'm *supposed* to do. And I understand, from what others may or may not have said while standing in that same spot, smiling curtly—it is obvious not much is *concrete* about any of this. What I care about is what *you* think. You are the man that I have served and the man that has led this church as the youth pastor for ten years. I don't care if not everyone thinks I can do this, or if they even try to take it from me. *I won't fail.* Because I know who I am and I know I'm supposed to do this. Everyone may be against me, but I just need to know— What do *you* say?"

When I heard those words come out of me, I realized what I was actually fighting and that I had somehow found exactly what I needed to defeat it. I didn't need everyone's approval. I just needed one man's. I didn't even need a title. I just needed to know I was supposed to do this, and who was giving it to me.

Bryan gave me his blessing *again*. All the while expressing that, like any change in authority and leadership, some people will always feel apprehension, fear and even anger, but as long as we keep our focus ahead and know who God says we are, we can keep moving and the rest will follow.

It reminded me that we are not up against flesh and blood. And that it truly is best for you and me to know our position, regardless of the world knowing or not. A title in the world is nothing, gone in an instant. But I am Keith, son of God, and you also, are a son or daughter of God, King of the Universe. That title can never be stripped away; the rest will follow.

On the other side of being planted and ordained in my position, I realized that all of it was nonsense thrown from the Enemy to make me afraid, jealous, angry or prideful, anything to knock me off course. There was no one against me; there were no hidden agendas (well, maybe *some*, but that's between them and God). Finding satisfaction in who God called me far outweighed what may or may not have been said behind my back.

The same for you! Every position of authority, power and influence comes with opposition. And your radical notion of what people *think* about you and *say* about you behind your back will personify itself into an ugly demon called Pride that will eat your lunch and pop the bag against your head. Shame comes from the feeling of unworthiness brought upon by missteps in the dark. Pride comes from the desire to mask ourselves or else just maybe everyone will realize, we too, have dirt on our faces. In this, they are cousins, that both Shame and Pride are the product of us knowing and believing: *we are failures.*

Marvin's pride that drove him to pick up a bag of feed with his teeth and nearly break his spine in half, was not brought on by a righteous necessity to teach those men they were incorrect in their assumption of what kind of man he was. No, his pride was generated from the feeling that deep inside of him, he wondered if what they said were true, and he was too scared to find out. This is why those that have their confidence founded on what God says about them really are the least prideful of all. I need not convince you nor myself I can do *everything*, because I know I can do what I am supposed to do *the best*.

This is why the idea that someone can "steal" your destiny is so absurd. God knows exactly who He is dealing with, and it is His choice, and His choice alone, of whom He will appoint, and whom He will put down. Our moving away from fear and pride, into rest and faith, allows Him to appoint us sooner.

In Genesis, Joseph knew what was destined for him.[2] But he was so afraid deep down that he may lose it, that he forced himself to parade his destiny and "talents" over others for most of his early life. In this, his acquisition of that destiny was delayed again and again through turmoil and defeat. God was always with him, but his arrogance chained him on more than one occasion.[3] It wasn't until he learned that he really had zero power and that only God was interpreting the dreams, did he finally walk into the fullness of what God had for him.[4] His humility propelled him, while his arrogance delayed him.

In Judges, Samson was born with a destiny to save Israel from the powers of darkness once and for all.[5] But his insecurity as a man and future husband[6] was so prolific, he would throw tantrums, act deviously, and intermingle with demonic harlots[7]. His pride swelled so extensively that he actually believed and confessed his strength came from his hair rather than the Spirit of God[8]. It wasn't until he was chained, blind and humiliated that he repented and cried out to God to fulfill his purpose of eradicating the Enemy—and even still it took his life[9]. His humility fulfilled his purpose, while his pride destroyed him.

ii. simple forgiveness and understanding

"Perfection is terrible; it cannot have children."
- Sylvia Plath

We all are to blame; all of us have dirt on our faces and blood on our hands. We have all fallen short of what is God's glory, all taking part in nailing Jesus to the cross with our sins[10]. But it's not the accumulation of mankind's sin that put Him on the cross; it was *one* sin, just as much as it was *all* of our sins. Your piddly amount of anger, fear, or pride earlier today was enough to kill Him. And whatever amount of doubt and faithlessness you had this afternoon buried Him.

However, quite remarkably God the Father chooses to look at us differently. He looks past the imperfection and sees someone He can use to do great and mighty things to create history. He looks at us like He looked at Peter, and sees a worthy and powerful apostle, while all the rest of his comrades only saw a fisherman with his foot in his mouth. And so He forgives us, choosing to forget our offense, while using our past, to propel us toward His perfect plan for our lives.

Forgiveness is a foreign concept for us, in every aspect of the word. *Foreign*—meaning it is from another country other than our own, God's country. It is not a natural occurrence or response. Nothing in the animal kingdom forgives; betrayal is met with violence and abandonment. Only after submission beats into the wolf is he allowed to fall back into the pack; only after the challenging bull elephant has left the parade will the rest of the family rest. And frankly, the submission of the wolf has little to do with honor, and more with waiting for the next opportunity. Forgiveness is not in us; it's from the stars.

Why on earth then do we find it flabbergasting when we are reminded just how difficult it is to forgive? Haven't we learned by now that we are trying to accomplish the impossible? The act of acquitting someone of all judgment for the felony they have created is damnable; every sin is worthy of death, whether great or small. Our lives are strung together by offense after unfair wrongdoing, yet we somehow learn to cope and coexist in this process of "that's just how life is".

And it's in this unspoken ideal that *forgiveness* is only another act of humanity—"something we are *just* supposed to do"—though it is something that is truly unnatural. Most likely, it comes upon us, by the recurring guidance and admonition of a parent telling us to both apologize and forgive as children. And more often than not, we aren't treated to the revelation that this act—*forgiveness*—is something no one was ever *naturally* made to do. Forgiveness is God's identity; therefore, it lies in the preternatural, outside of our day-to-day and brushing-teeth routine.

And so, with this deep-rooted idea that we are "*supposed*" to forgive, coupled with the lack of understanding that we can't do this without God's presence, we try our best in life to "forgive and forget", until the moment comes that we are truly betrayed, hurt or abused. And at that moment, we throw up our hands, committing ourselves to extreme bitterness and un-forgiveness—it's not that we can't forgive them, now it is that we wish we never met, or worse, that they never existed.

Our belief that *forgiveness* is something we just *do*, catalyzes our bitterness and frustration when we realize we *can't*. Without the Spirit of God's direction, knowing full well the offender doesn't "deserve" it, it is impossible to forgive.

Do they deserve forgiveness? Of course, not! No one *deserves* forgiveness because it's not a natural occurrence. What we deserve is death.[11] God forgave us at our lowest moment; Jesus died for us, taking all our deserved eternal suffering.

Should we forgive? Of course! If for no other reason then because Christ forgave us.[12] He has implanted His character into us, and just as Romans 12 states, we are working continually to be transformed more into Jesus, by the changing of our minds.[13] We are not like the world any longer; therefore, we do not act *natural* anymore;[14] we are *super*-natural.

When we can understand that God's perfect will for our lives involves us learning to forgive, even at its hardest moments, we will see that we, in fact, aren't stuck in life because we *can't* forgive; we are stuck because we *won't* forgive.

Most of us misconstrue what forgiveness is. We hear phrases like "forgive and forget", and immediately think, "there is no way I could forgive *that* person because I will never forget what they did to me." But forgiveness is not bridging a relationship after blindly forgetting your hurt, thus, making you susceptible to more torment or abuse—it is simply the act of letting go of someone's throat.

Amazingly, as we practice the works of God's character, we see that we become more like Him, and every day, it is simpler and simpler to continue this faith practice. Forgiving others becomes a new part of who we are, as we become more like Christ. And though, some offenses may take longer to let go of, all can be accomplished through His Spirit.

Note, that while the initial *forgiving* of someone may be a simple statement and belief, the walking out of that faith (just like any other) may take time, even years to accomplish fully. But if we will continue to release our grip from around that person's neck, openly reminding ourselves that we have indeed forgiven them, we will see our bitterness disappear and our offense dissolve. The hurt may never go away, but we will be free of the bondage it brings us.

Bitterness, unforgiveness and pride are verily nothing more than the acts of a child who refuses to say "I'm sorry" and be friends, in exchange for the promise of being able to play again or eat its dinner. Only this child has "grown up" and found how to play alone or make its own meal. The unforgiveness is still just as childish, but the immediate threat has been removed, rendering the adult even more stupid somehow. Thus, we find age does not propagate maturity, only experience. We haven't really grown up if we are still holding onto unforgiveness; we are just older children that don't have a parent to tell us we are being selfish.

We cannot write people off in our lives, even due to betrayal. Jesus is our example here, in that he was betrayed again and again by those closest to Him, and yet somehow embodied forgiveness, allowing them back into His life and giving them great purpose.

On the night of His death, Jesus was betrayed once by Judas, and thrice by Peter. Judas was led by a demonic possession and greed that twisted his mind out of control and reason. Peter was led by a fear that caused him to doubt his faith and love in Jesus.

Oftentimes in life, we assume people's wrongdoing toward us is because of some deep-rooted evil inside of them. But more often than not, and frankly *every* time I have ever counseled someone, we discover that people's selfish and sinful actions are the product of fear, rather than innate evil.

When people lie, it's because they are afraid the truth will bring them punishment or lose them someone's trust; when they steal, they are afraid they will never have enough; when they cheat, they are afraid they aren't capable or talented enough to make it the honest way; when they are unfaithful to a spouse, it's because they are afraid that spouse won't love or satisfy them the way they desire; when they intoxicate themselves, it's from a fear they won't find joy or satisfaction any other way; when they are proud, it's because they fear they won't matter without their own boasting. Sin is the product of fear.

Upon realizing that a person's treachery has little in common with a sadistic and malevolent spirit, and more in common with an abandoned child, we find it easier to forgive. Stop holding someone's offense toward you as a judge and start viewing it as a cry for help.

Now, of course, again, I'm not advocating we openly allow ourselves to be walked over, used and abused by any individual that so attempts. What did Jesus do with Peter, after his betrayal? He had breakfast with him. He restored his soul. He asked him again and again where his allegiance lay, and if he loved Him. It wasn't until two months after Peter's conviction and repentance that Jesus began using him to do great and powerful things for the Church again.

So should we follow the example: release the neck; restore the relationship; empower the individual. If they are unwelcome to restoring the relationship, then it waits in limbo** until the day of growth and maturation.[15]

Remember, your season doesn't determine your story. Regardless of where you find yourself today in your ability, sin, or unforgiveness toward others, everything can change in an instant by

---

** *word used metaphorically only.*

you choosing to live like a *legend*. Nothing holds you back from becoming that, except yourself.

iii. the trap of not letting go

"Nothing that you have not given away
will ever be really yours."
- C. S. Lewis

When Carlia was pregnant with Harvey, we changed hospitals. He was born at Parrish Medical Center in Titusville, FL. It was a hospital much further from our hometown; thus, a more unlikely place for people to visit us. That wasn't the reason we changed hospitals, but it was a repercussion of the act. Nonetheless, one individual (let's call her Rebecca) found her way out to visit us on the day after Harvey's birth, to congratulate us and have an impromptu counseling session in the hospital room, right next to my sleeping wife and son.

Rebecca was one of our students that had recently graduated and was now a leader on our youth ministry team. Her concern was that she and some of her close friends were at odds more and more frequently about how they should spend time together. Not too long ago, their group occasionally acted as many adolescents—they would find humor in the surreal, and cruelly point out people's faults from a distance. They weren't altogether *bad* in any way whatsoever; in fact, they were great students that loved Jesus and loved people; they just enjoyed having cynicism in their hearts— *who doesn't right?!*

But in Rebecca's heart, something was changing. As her relationship with Jesus grew, so did her perspective of others that she did not know. She didn't see them as potential jokes any longer, but as God's children. When other's in her group wanted to make fun of the manic homeless man, she desired to speak to him, perhaps bring him some food and the love of God. This put her contrary to the desires of her group. They began deriding Rebecca for "looking down" on the rest, acting high-and-mighty, and professed her a hypocrite because she would have done the same thing only two weeks before.

Now she was at a crossroads, stuck in transition. Should she stay with her group and give up on growing? Should she continue to grow and leave behind these naysayers? Or were they right—was she nothing but a hypocrite?

Few of us keep the same friend(s) throughout our entire life. I am one of the lucky that have known closely my dear friend Joshua Ellis our entire lives. Our friendship started when we were only 18 months old and we still do regular life together as best friends and confidants. We work out together; we serve together; we pray together. Even our wives and children are best friends. Other than that though, my friendships, like all of us, have grown and wilted based on proximity, age, and interest.

What happens in ministry life, as Christians serving the Lord and the local church, is that we find a group of friends and believers that we confide in and love doing life alongside. They become our *tribe*. We have the same interests, hobbies, friends, and ideals. We may work on the same serve teams and hang out together at the local *Steak 'N' Shake*[††].

But eventually, maybe years down the road and not without purposeful decisions made in individual lives, we separate from that group or that person. It's not that we don't enjoy their presence anymore, or even that we don't *want* to spend time with them. It's simply that the flow of life pulls all of us different directions and

---

[††] does anyone still eat there?

our own intelligence or maturation decides how quickly or slowly we move in it.

Of course, I'm not describing some sort of altercation between the two parties that makes them refuse to be brothers or sisters any longer. And I'm absolutely not painting a picture that people should abandon their local church over a squabble or a "change of heart". I'm only describing the natural flow of life and how we make little adjustments along the way that amount to a large gap in the future. And when we look over our shoulder, we realize our friend is no longer there and that we haven't even recognized their departure, only because we realize we haven't needed them.

It's similar to the experience of moving out of your parent's home as you grow out of adolescence. Of course, in that scenario, there is a very deliberate departure and therefore a very deliberate goodbye. But if we were honest with ourselves, the majority of us move out of our parent's home mentally before physically. And this is my point: few of us leave our parents angry and with this so-called "change of heart". We move out because it's the natural flow of life.

Even in my friendship with Josh, we have ebbed and flowed in and out of one another's lives. There were moments through high school and college, and again in adult life, that our choices, desires, or the will of God led us in different directions. For us, those moments were relatively brief and we would find ourselves connected again in some fashion and excited to do life with one another.

What can happen to Christians that have found a very strong tribe, but are feeling pulled other directions or are less and less interested in the goals or desires of their group, is that they feel a sense of guilt shadowed by their longing to follow God's Spirit and His will for their lives. This can make the process slow and painful.

One side of them wants to listen to the Holy Spirit and move with abandonment, but the other side feels guilty for not spending enough time with their tribe. And now they find themselves attracted to a *new* tribe with different people.

Firstly, just because your tribe is less attractive doesn't mean you consider them less worthy. The Apostle Paul and Barnabas separated ways in Acts 15 because Paul didn't trust the apostle Mark's loyalty[16] but Barnabas wanted him there. It separated the friends. Was either of them any less used by God afterward? No! Were either of them in sin for their disagreement or separation? Not likely.

Paul and Peter's friendship shook when Peter wanted to focus his attention solely on the Jewish nation, and Paul primarily wanted to seek after the Gentiles.[17] The two men separated in their quests to sharing the Gospel with the world. Both men did incredible things for Jesus. Both men did it with different tribes.

Sometimes when we are in ministry together, we think it must be wrong to move on from the tribes and groups of people we are with. After all, we are the *body of Christ*! How can we separate from one another?

But the separation of interest and proximity is not the same as the separation of mission and purpose. If the Spirit of God calls us different directions, we should listen. However, if that direction leads us away from those we have confided in and away from the place we have rooted ourselves for the last decade, we should be careful to walk in wisdom and clarity. Seek counsel from leadership, pastors, and friends. Don't make rash decisions based on excitement and the "moving of the Spirit".‡‡

---

‡‡ Too many Christians have walked into sin, loneliness or financial turmoil because they confused excitement and license for the Holy Spirit.

The everyday tides of life are constantly taking you a direction, and you may look around one day and realize you are not the same person you were two years ago and don't have the same friends you had five years ago. This is a good and holy thing if you are continually seeking the will of God.

And amazingly enough, God is able to bring people back into your life that you thought gone forever. Paul and Barnabas reconciled; Paul could even work with Mark again.[18] Peter admitted his wrong in only caring about the Jew and not the Gentile, praising Paul for his works.[19] This is why we walk by the Spirit of forgiveness and not our own judgment.

So I told Rebecca that her tribe was changing, which doesn't mean she's a bad person and it doesn't mean they are bad people. I also warned her against the temptation to believe that just because she was evolving into a new person didn't mean that she was somehow *better* than the rest.

We all have our strengths and weaknesses in the Body of Christ, and while some of us may grow and say yes to God quicker and sooner than others, it doesn't mean we are elite over, or more special than, the rest. At any point, any of us could fly forward in our growth by revelation and commitment, and at any point, any of us could fall down to the depths by sin and complacency. What's important is knowing that the Holy Spirit, and only the Holy Spirit, is who makes us important.

iv. judging others and ourselves properly

"What a man does defiles him, not what is done by others."
- William Golding

All of mankind's faith and journey are defined by different factors and occurrences, whether they involve upbringing, opportunity, choice, or sin. And no one person can look at another and fully understand the factor needed to make or break someone from a powerful future. In fact, most legendary actions are birthed from the vessel of simple and seemingly uncomplicated decisions surrounded by an ocean of potentially foolish and even selfish ones.

Humans are absolutely terrible at judging others with a base appraisal. We assume and prejudge one another and compare their accolades to our own before we even learn someone's full name. Though we should all be striving for the same goal of greatness in Christ Jesus, our current status may seem very diverse than that of others.

Thank God, He is Judge![20]

If I were, too many of the wrong people would be in Christ's office, and I would overlook too many that have great things ahead of them. Not all are leaders, *though all should be*. And nothing on the outside of the heart can fully determine what makes a leader; thus, God is the Judge of hearts.[21]

For some, the act of going from nine packs of cigarettes a day to three is a victory unlike any other. If my focus is only on my own victories, and they are the scales I use to judge, I can miss the miracles happening in other's lives that *weigh* differently, thus robbing myself of experiencing their testimony and being a part of their history.

Your victories look different from that of others. No one, on this side of eternity, can judge another man's worship, another man's moral compass, or another man's process. Only God can judge and know those things intimately. When you see others, don't look past their process, or yours will be looked past.

Now, of course, the fruit of a man's actions reveals his heart[22]. Therefore, I am able to see another man's outcome and make an assessment of his heart and soul, whether good or bad. But even in that, I fall short in knowing the true intent or motivation of the heart. Many good men and women do evil things being led by fear or rejection. All have fallen short of the glory of God, and all of us need His grace to survive. When we compare, we sin. When we judge that we are greater than another, we fall short of greatness ourselves.

Now, of course, we should judge other's circumstances. Without that, without knowing they are sick, I am unable to administer health. Matthew 7 does not rebuke us for judging another person's life in order that we may help them or even that we wouldn't allow them to potentially hurt someone weaker or younger; it rebukes the notion that we would deem someone unsalvageable and thus, damn them.[23]

Paul writes to the Corinth Church that "there are diversities of gifts, but the same Spirit"[24] and that "the same Spirits works all these things, distributing each one individually as He wills."[25] I believe the Holy Spirit has a sick sense of humor for making sure we rely on one another for His will to be fulfilled. Because God will not use one person to change the world. He will use all of His persons, and if we could grasp this true understanding, stop fighting about who is the greatest,[26] and start running the race as hard as we can,[27] we would see His will be done on earth as it is in heaven.

The Spirit of God moves across the earth, fervently hunting for any believer to call upon Him and act in faith. Nothing from you, but your belief and movement, determine a miracle. The gifts of the Spirit are the gifts *of* the Spirit. Not *from* the Spirit. They are *His* yesterday, today and tomorrow. Our haughty sense of entitlement is only birthed by the idea that we have obtained these gifts. In fact, we have only obtained the Holy Spirit, and He is working through us. And He will work whichever gift through whichever believer He so desires.

This is why you have prayed for someone's healing and saw it happen before your eyes, only to be disappointed at the next juncture. Because it's not your gift; it's the Holy Spirit's. And His desire is that we, the children of God, would come together, working in one accord, administering the will of God as He administers the power of God. And until we come together in one voice, putting aside pride and prejudice, we will not see that perfect will of God, and in effect, will not experience our lives leaving a legacy of legend.

Without the Spirit, humans are only a body and soul. We are equivalent to a cat, dog or primate. Ironically, the very thing that the evolutionist has claimed about their connection to the animal kingdom is very accurate indeed.

But we were never intended to be that way; we were meant to be alive in our spirit and different from anything that has ever walked this earth. Instead of recognizing their fullest potential, the evolutionist has stunted their growth, by not allowing the concept of a spirit they need, in order to live the life they were intended. The further we get from being led by God's Spirit, the closer we get to self-fulfilling the evolutionist's prophecy of being nothing but an animal.

And so, humans dance on the outer edges of God's perfect will. The pagan claims we are nothing more than animals, and while rejecting the Spirit of God, becomes one. The haughty self-righteous Christian looks down on his brothers, entitling himself to all the gifts of the Spirit, and thus, is refused them.

But if only we could understand this glimmer of truth that changing the world requires us to live our time in between two very specific mindsets—knowing fully that all of our effort and work in our little lives will not amount to a hill of beans in the grand scheme of creation and eternity; while also understanding that it is our sole duty, requirement and passion to exhaust ourselves at saving every last person and making this place in to heaven—if we could see that divine dichotomy, we would see our purpose. None of this matters. And all of this matters.

v. Marvin's pride abandoned

For seven years, Marvin walked in sin. He refused to go near any House of God. But his rejection of the holy and righteous was only the product of deep down knowing he was wrong, and his silly pride was keeping him from admitting it.

During the seventh summer of Marvin's recklessness, Mamie begged him to come to Camp Meeting with their family. The Church of God Camp Meeting was a week of worship and revival, deep in the south near Ruskin, FL at Wimauma. Over 10,000 spirit-filled Christians would gather at the tabernacle to sing praises together, eat food, and hear from the leaders of God's Church. Every year, Mamie would take her four kids to Camp Meeting. And every year Marvin would refuse to go, though he would drive the family to it.

The Alderman's had become poor in Marvin's pride. Their vehicle was nothing more than a rusty block on wheels that cantankerously waddled down the highway. The kids in the back seat could actually see the road racing underneath through the missing floorboard.

Along the way, the family stopped at a food stand selling watermelon. Mamie and Lewis chatted with the vender, as Marvin stood at the edge of the road with Leland. Betty was wandering off into the field nearby. Little Nona was sleeping in the back of the car, her head between her knees.

Marvin watched his son, Leland, who was holding a piece of watermelon in one hand, and with the other was chasing a small wolf spider creeping along the rocky earth. He smiled at his boy, that was on the very edge of being a man. He looked up to see Betty, twirling in the grass, and chasing grasshoppers and butterflies. His eyes caught his bride's for a moment, though her smile broke his gaze. He looked to the car and saw Nona in the backseat.

"Nona," he hollered. "Get out here and eat some watermelon! It's going to be a couple more hours before we are there."

Nona did not stir. He hollered again.

Concern crossed Mamie's face as she took a step toward the car; she could feel fear creeping down her spine.

"Marvin…" her voice was shaky.

As she approached the car, Nona's color was visibly white. Marvin was there too, holding her wrist in his hand. Leland picked up the spider on a rock. Betty fell down in the grass, twisting her ankle and letting out a yelp. Marvin began shaking Nona by the shoulders, calling her name for her to wake up. Her head fell forward by the violence of his jerk. Leland threw the rock as far as he could.

"What's wrong with her, Marvin!" Mamie cried out, trying to keep herself composed.

What was wrong with her was, that for the two hours the Alderman's drove along the dirt highway, carbon monoxide was filtering its way up through the floorboard of the vehicle. And little Nona, who had laid down to nap next to her siblings, had been steadily consuming the gas. She was no longer breathing.

"I don't know—" Marvin replied.

"—What do you mean?" Mamie hollered. "Do something! Make her come back!"

"I'm trying!" Marvin snapped back. He pulled Nona from the car and laid her at the side of the road. "Nona! Wake up, sweetie!" He frantically patted Nona's face, more and more violently.

"Pray for her, Marvin!" Mamie ordered. "Pray to God and make her come back to life!"

It stunned him as a deer in headlights. He couldn't move. He couldn't think. He forgot how to believe.

"Pray for her!" Mamie ordered again.

"I...I can't..." he whispered. He let go of his daughter and slunk away in shame.

Mamie was in shock. How could her husband be the man that raised a woman from the dead, now unable to pray for his own daughter?

Marvin walked a few feet off into a nearby field. His head hung low in shame and anger. He wanted to be mad at God, but he was only mad at himself. Seven years of ignoring God and hating the Church turned him into an ineffectual wimp of a man.

Mamie ignored her husband's foolishness and immediately began praying over Nona. "In the name of Jesus, I command you to wake up!" She spoke to Nona. "Please God—Wake up my baby girl..."

Leland, Betty and Lewis were there now, standing close by in silence and fear. They couldn't move. One moment was the brief and rare occurrence of joy and playfulness; the next was one of grief and terror.

"Please God!" Mamie continued. "Please wake up my baby! Wake up in Jesus' name!"

Cough. Cough.

Nona coughed, and a nasty black cloud came from her lungs; she opened her eyes. Mamie embraced her, crying.

"Oh thank you, Jesus," she whispered. Nona sat up in her mother's arms as the rest of her siblings held her. Marvin ran to be by her side, astonished. But he could not hug her.

The family finally made it the rest of the way and were in Wimauma. As Mamie took the four kids under the massive pavilion, Marvin stayed back under the night sky, staring forward at the immense group of believers worshiping God. He could see Ray Hughes, who would later become the General Overseer of the Church of God, preaching at the podium. He was shouting from the front to 10,000 people why the blood of Jesus can cover any sin and forgive any fault—it only takes our "yes and amen".

Marvin looked up at the stars. It was the same sky that he once saw the Old and New Testament written in the clouds. It was the same sky that hung over him when he preached. It was the same sky that was always with him, and would never leave him.

He heard a voice speak loud and clear to him.

"Marvin, will you serve me?"

He refused to speak. His pride had turned to nothing but guilt. He no longer believed he deserved to go back to God.

"Marvin...if you leave Me now, you won't live for another chance."

He boldly looked up at the Camp and took a step forward. It was the first step that was the hardest, but as soon as he felt his body give way and decide to move, the rest of his soul followed, and he rushed into the body of believers.

He immediately walked to the very front, stepped onto the wooden stage, and approached Ray. Ray knew who he was; everyone knew who he was. This was Marvin Alderman, and he was finally home.

"May I speak?" Marvin asked Ray.

Ray nodded at him and moved away from the pulpit.

With tears running down his face, Marvin addressed the 10,000 men, women, and children. "I dishonored God," he said. "I dishonored the Church. I was wrong. And I want all of you to know I'm sorry. I'm sorry for how many people have gone to Hell because of me..." His face fell down in sorrow and grief. "—If you'll receive me back, I'll give you my level best for the rest of my life."

Ray Hughes wrapped both of his arms around him. "In our eyes," he spoke loud enough for all to hear. "...you never left, brother."

After 17 years in ministry, pride took Marvin away. After seven years of sin, humility brought him back. The year was 1953. He would serve as a minister of the Church of God for the final 17 years of his life.

vi. God calling

"There will always be a fight
against our culture's values and our sinful nature.
We can't afford to go with the flow. We have to be intentional."
- Samuel Chand

God doesn't call forever. Now before I am chastised for saying something so legalistic and "un-grace-filled" as God doesn't call people forever, I hope I can express the difference between someone called to *salvation*, and someone called to a *legend*.

We define our lives each and every day by the small choices, thoughts and beliefs we make. And yes, we thrust forward, or temper back, into the future of greatness, or insignificance, based on that definition. Mordecai told Esther that if she failed to stand and be great, God would bring an answer through someone else, and she would die.[28] If you have things deep inside of you coming to life and burning to get out—things like integrity, risk, and perseverance —the time is now to activate them and begin using them for God's kingdom. And yes, those things will disappear if you let them, as will the impact you have on this earth.

In our western American culture, we are entirely misguided in our belief that life is about our happiness and peace, and that we will get a thousand second-chances. For decades, we have been sold the picture that a new product, drug, or sexual adventure will satisfy us, and nothing else matters except that unattainable satisfaction. Nowhere else on the planet, culture or time has this been the case. Life is not meant to be easy; it's meant to be meaningful.

Of course, I believe God's salvation is available always,[29] and his mercies are new each morning. There *are* a thousand second-chances (in this life) to reach out and accept Jesus as Lord and Savior. But we aren't discussing acceptance here; we are discussing influence. No amount of greatness ever came without a great amount of sacrifice. Your *legend* is on the other side of much pain, failure, desperation, and heartache. That's what makes it a *legend*. And that's what makes *you* the only one able to go and obtain it.

Greatness comes with consequence, and it's a choice to walk through that consequence. Are you able to walk fully aware, with an unequivocal yes, into the future of pain and sacrifice, with the end in sight, amidst the journey of both failure and success? If you can say yes to that question, then you can become a *legend*.

But know beyond any doubt that God doesn't call you forever into this. Your haphazard and reluctant steps will only dissolve the dreams and goals ahead of you, all the while making the stories behind you less meaningful. No one can steal your destiny *except you*.

If you have breath in your lungs and a dream in your heart, aim at it now. If you have an ounce of wisdom in your mind, share it now. If you have a glimmer of adventure left in your bones, take it now. We have the choice before each of us today—to live a life of true meaning, great difficulty and plenty of pain, or to live a life of mediocrity and self-satisfaction.

From what I can discern in the Holy text, there are little consequences to this decision, whether you take the life of legend or the life of unremarkable. Both with Jesus will see the pearly gates. Though, I'm not confident the latter will hear the words, "Well done, good and faithful servant" and instead only, "Well…you're done." I personally refuse to *just get by*.

Of course, I doubt you would be reading this book if you disagreed with me at this point. So instead, I pose another question to you; one that is perhaps more painful and hard to succumb.

What if we aren't all supposed to be great?

The problem with humans is that we look at differences as a method to weigh and measure value. God looks at differences as a method to share beauty and creativity. So while we see someone with a different gift, we elevate or lower that person according to our own limited perspective; meanwhile, God wishes we would stop measuring and start celebrating. This is why He reminds us that, "there are different kinds of service, but it is the same God who does the work in all of us."[30]

We aren't meant to be *great*, by definition, better than *others*. We are meant to be *great*, in the sense of—the greatest versions of *ourselves*. And if and when we can accomplish this feat together, we will resemble the Bride of Christ better than ever. The disciples argued on Jesus' final night before his execution, about which of them was the greatest—to which He responded, "He that takes the lowest rank."[31]

We aren't meant to be famous among men. We are meant to make Jesus famous among men. We are only the vessels that choose to allow Him to be great in our lives. None of this is about us; it is about *all of us*. Alone, we are less. Together, we are great. So neither I nor you can judge what a good and faithful life of adventure and purpose really looks like because it looks different to everyone but the Father. And that's why it's His joy to say those words, and not ours.

When Jesus calls us to become His children, He then calls us to become His disciples. And it's in leaving everything behind and truly trusting Him with everything that we find our purpose and *greatness*; it's in this we find our *legend*. And whether or not we are remembered by the billions like Billy Graham, or by one lone last great-grandson like Marvin Alderman, we will be remembered in God's bright and shining eyes as nothing less than *legends*. In His fame is where we find our standing place.

Remember, in the story of Decapolis, Jesus instructed the disciples to cross to the other side in order to find a man chained to the cliffs. He was a demoniac that, upon receiving his salvation, would go on to lead many to the feet of Jesus with his testimony. The disciples were first called to enter the boat, next to survive the storm, and finally to rescue this man.

Jesus calls us to greatness, though we rarely feel great. Even less do we feel we are amid something great. But in the fruit of our pain and disappointment—our passionate laboring—is something that will be talked about for centuries.

When you are called, as they were called, say yes.

When you are in the boat, making the journey through storms and fear of death, have faith.

When you are at the cliffs, just as the demoniac ran and bowed before the King of kings, worship your God.

My great-grandfather Marvin Alderman said yes to God many times over. And his journey led him through many terrible storms, the greatest being when his own pride led him through years of rebellion and sin. But at the tent, he could worship again. And likewise to his story, we all need to understand that true repentance is much less a saying *no* to some contrary life of sin, and much more a *yes* to the living God.

Some of us are embarking, some of us are amidst storms, and some of us are in over our heads. The response is always *yes*, *faith*, and *worship*.

Even if it's the last thing we do.

PART 5 :
Even if It's the Last Thing We Do

"If you make yourself more than just a man.
If you devote yourself to an ideal, and if they can't stop you,
then you become something else entirely—a legend. *"*

- Ducard, Batman Begins[1]

i. what legends bear

We are not perfect, though we strive to be. Our bodies will require more food and rest. Our souls will require recharging. Our flesh will be selfish. Our emotions will be reckless. We are *not* perfect. The striving for perfection will destroy us if we rely only on ourselves. Nevertheless, the legendary spirit will always desire more. Remember: God doesn't call the special; He calls the *crazy*. That's what makes a legend worth telling.

To my understanding, there are undoubtedly three types of Christians. Christ refers to us as a family, and as such, I will label us blatantly. In our families, there are *babies, adults,* and *parents.*

Christian Babies, like infants, cry aloud every moment something doesn't go as they intend or hope. You have seen these people; those that cry for others to spoon-feed them the Word while refusing to learn how to hold it, in order to feed themselves. And if you put some peas in their soup or stretch their theology, they refuse to eat it: *"nuh-uh!"* because *"it doesn't taste good."*

When they fall down, they expect others to pick them back up, and will only continue to whine and moan until somehow has. When they crap their pants with sin, they continue to walk around in it until someone cleans them up.

And God forbid He put them in time-out or they will run to their room screaming like they lost a limb. Every blessing must be *now*, and every thing must be *for them*! These are the babies that Paul wrote about in 1 Corinthians, chapter three, when he stated, *"I had to talk as though you belonged to this world or as though you were infants in Christ. I had to feed you with milk, not with solid food, because you weren't ready for anything stronger."[2]*

Of course, my playful irritation with infants is obvious, and that is because I have had three to manage personally as a father. I have changed hundreds of diapers and put up with countless tantrums about toys being taken away after a said child hit their sister in the face with said toy. But I also understand the enormity and vital importance that the *Baby* brings to the family. The Baby brings life, purpose, youth, and legacy. Without the Baby, the family name would not carry on, and as such, we would disappear. We need to constantly reproduce ourselves in the family of Christ. Without the Baby, adults would become complacent, elitist, and proper; and frankly, Jesus Christ is nothing like that. Life is not about us; it's about the furthering of the kingdom of God, and that begins with Babies.

We all were Babies once, and thus, we have grace and understanding for the Baby. We all have expected everyone else to tell us what to do next; we all have waited for Jesus to fix all of our problems; we all have cried in sorrow, waiting for life to suddenly get easier.

But my children should not stay babies. I expect them to grow, listen and learn. One day they will feed and provide for themselves.

When they are hungry, they will stand up, walk to the pantry, and prepare a sandwich. They will become *Adults.*

In actuality, an adult doesn't just walk to the pantry and prepare a sandwich. The Adult knows that without preparation, the needed ingredients will not be present in the kitchen. Therefore, the Adult goes to work. He or she makes the money or resources necessary to prepare a meal *before they even need it.*

Paul describes this person in Hebrews, chapter five, when he says, *"For someone who lives on milk is still an infant and doesn't know how to do what is right. Solid food is for those who are mature, who through* training *have the skill to recognize between right and wrong."[3]* There is clearly a correlation between what the Christian is capable of and their reward, just as an adult both experiences more responsibility *and freedom* than a child or infant.

Paul continues, *"So let us stop going over the* basic teachings *about Christ again and again. Let us go on instead and become* mature *in our understanding. Surely we don't need to start again with the fundamental importance of repenting from evil deeds and placing our faith in God. You don't need further instruction about baptisms, the laying on of hands, the resurrection of the dead, and eternal judgment. And so, God willing, we will move forward to further understanding."[4]*

I relate and understand Paul's frustration with the Hebrew Church, one that he no doubt believed should be further along than any other Gentile gathering. And yet, he must repeat himself endlessly about the base and fundamental beliefs on baptisms, healings, raising the dead to life, and what eternity looks like. Meanwhile, many of us today are walking around drinking our milk and wondering if Christ really wants us to pray for the sick and raise the dead! These are *base* and *fundamental* lessons of the Christian faith. It is apparent, *at least to me*, that many of us are far from what Paul would consider an *Adult Christian.*

Can we, *please*, move on to *further understanding?* Can we stop getting hung up and out of sorts on whether we should repent from our sins and have faith?

We should understand baptism, both of the physical and spiritual. We should understand the power of laying hands on someone in prayer and faith. We should know, believe, and experience the resurrection of the dead in Christ Jesus, and our eternal judgment with Him. We should move on to further understanding.

And finally, we should prepare our meals before we are hungry. Some of us work weeks in advance of the natural food we will eat with the money we have raised. And yet many of us are running to the Word only when life gets hard, or are giving up on faith altogether, with our hands raised in the air and our screams to the heavens, nothing more than a *Baby* would.

There is one more character in our family of Christ. And that is the role that the Apostle Paul himself wore. It's actually what many bear, but few mention, because those that model this role only ever intend to publicly teach the *Babies* and *Adults*; whilst they themselves teach one another privately (at least on a grand and large scale). It's what creates discipleship and apprenticeship, through the work of one not being satisfied with being fed, or even feeding themselves. This individual works so that others can eat. I am speaking of course, about the family role of *Parent.*

Parents feed the *Babies* and train them on how to become *Adults.* It's what Paul referenced in his first letter to the Corinthians, chapter four, *"I am not writing these things to shame you, but to warn you as* my beloved children. *For even if you had ten thousand others to teach you about Christ, you have only one spiritual* father. *For I became your father in Christ Jesus when I preached the Good News to you. So I urge you to imitate me.*"[5]

Most of the food in my house, I never get to eat. I work so that others (my wife and children) can eat. Parents go beyond working and preparing meals for themselves; they are preparing meals for the hungry and weak; working hard to stay ahead of everyone else's problems.

But, you say, *that's not fair Keith! Why should I work so hard for the sniveling, whining little babies that never learned to grow up? They have been trapped in their same foolish sin, ceaselessly asking for handouts, and complaining about the Church for a decade! They don't deserve my time. I have more important things to do. Didn't you see them in the food pantry line whilst on their latest iPhone?! It's not fair; it's indecent. I will learn and grow and become something great. I haven't any time to waste on such selfish individuals. God has me for the lost and hurting, not the Pharisee and the hypocrite.*

To which I reply: Of course, it's not fair! And of course, you could live a happy life as an *Adult* Christian, loving Jesus, healing the sick, and helping the world. But I thought you wanted to become a *legend*. I thought you wouldn't settle at helping the world; you wanted to *change* it.

Paul, remember, changed his entire eating habits, not because it was a sin, but because it may have caused others to sin.[6] Is it fair? No! Is he a *legend*! Cursed be the man who thinks he isn't.

Are you preparing your own spiritual meals, or are you working diligently, bearing the mantle of *Parent*, found ready to feed someone else's soul when they come hungry? Are you throwing your net out "one more time"?

EVEN IF IT'S THE LAST THING WE DO

ii. what legends hear

"Freedom is not of use
to those who do not know how to employ it."
                                                    - Sylvia Plath

In 2018, a YouTube video containing nothing more than a simple audio sample went viral.[7] It contained a piece of slurred verbiage that many swore sounded like the word *laurel*, while others believed pronounced the word *yanny*. Debates broke out, food fights commenced, and the world stopped as everyone individually wondered if they were going insane, second-guessed whether they could hear correctly all their life, or were perhaps involved in one of the greatest and largest practical jokes of our generation. 53% of every human who heard this audio file heard the word *laurel*; 47% heard *yanny*.

In turns out, there is a simple science behind the misunderstood audio. There is only one word spoken, and the word is *laurel*. But it is spoken with higher frequencies overlaid, creating a strange effect that makes it sound as if it is a different word altogether. Depending upon what speakers and ears can project and detect, respectively, the sound will voice a different enunciation. If your phone speakers are poor or your headphones lack a higher frequency, you may hear a boomier low-end unction that sounds like the correct word *laurel*. If your speakers are better quality and able to reach higher spectrums, you may hear that the word has been manipulated into *yanny*.

However, more important than this factor is what you are actually capable of hearing. Someone with younger ears typically can hear higher frequencies, and thus, able to hear the distortion *yanny*. Someone with aged and damaged ears may only hear the original content of *laurel*. And even still, many hear opposing sounds at different instances, depending on what other noises and frequencies are floating around their ears in the natural ambiance of the room.

It seems what we are capable of hearing will determine how we interpret what is said. When Jesus said, *"You are truly my disciples if you remain faithful to my teachings. And you will know the truth, and the truth will set you free,"[8]* many interpret differing meanings to this statement, based solely upon what they are capable of hearing.

For instance, many hear conviction. The unbeliever hears nonsense or even condemnation. "What do you mean, 'I'm not free'?" they say. Because to them, the truth only traps them, and the idea of being a disciple of truth as the only means to salvation is narrow-minded and judgmental.

To the *Baby*, it's the excuse to demand everything while screaming. "You promised me freedom!" they cry. "Now give it to me!"

To the *Adult*, it's the excuse to take care of oneself and *exclusively* that oneself. "Jesus told all of you how to walk in freedom," they arrogantly ponder regarding others around. "Now pick yourselves up and act civilized, already."

And this is where humankind has tripped up many times. Those that have fought and died for freedom understand what it really is. But those that have inherited it typically think that freedom, by definition, is doing whatever they want.

Friar John Corapi once orated:

> *"Freedom is not being able to do whatever you want to do. That is* license. *If you have license, rather than authentic freedom, your house is built on sand and will collapse. Authentic freedom is the power to do what we* ought *to do; the power to*

choose the good, the true, and the beautiful. That will vanquish fear every time. If your concept of freedom is really license, fear will come out on top every time. Freedom has to be united with truth. There is no freedom outside of the truth: No authentic human freedom outside of the truth."

Truth will many times sound like nonsense, just as *yanny* and *laurel*. To one person, it may sound like one thing, and to another, they hear something else; all based upon what they are capable of hearing. Both swear the other is crazy and will die by what they believe. But truth does not change; its existence is not dependent on what we are or are not capable of understanding.

Truth, to the world, will never make sense; this is a constant, *"for only those who are spiritual can understand what the Spirit means."*[9] This is why you have experienced the frustrating and nerve-racking confabs with unbelievers who have the most difficult time understanding simple fundamental truths of God's Word. These people ask the most foolish questions and stare blankly at obvious reason, all the while calling you a fool for believing.

This is also why debate and argument rarely, if ever, yield the fruit of salvation. Because basic truth thrown in people's faces will not set people free; only the loving guidance of a friend and brother will. Jesus came to share relationships and stories with people; not read texts and scriptures at people's confused faces.

And in our own lack of understanding, we must go back to God's faith. When you do not understand everything written or everything experienced, understand, at least, that you aren't *meant* to understand everything. You are meant to trust God's truth. Faith comes first; understanding comes later.

And this leads us to the idea of philosophy and whether *it* also is fruitless. I would not suggest that it is foolhardy to ponder things like one's existence, the beginning and end of things, and what may or may not have happened in our creation. The Word of God does not fill in every detail, frankly, by design. Our imagination, questions, and ideas are things that God Himself created in us. And, as Lewis stated, we need *good* philosophy, if at least to correct *bad* philosophy.[10]

It's only when our philosophies, imaginations, and ideas grow larger than what the Word of God states or who the character of God is represented in Christ Jesus as, that we finally walk into a dangerous state of mind and act out in the demonic. The act itself of imagining and questioning is not bad, it's only the act of putting such imaginations greater than what God has given us and proven to be true that is truly *bad*. Philosophy can tempt us into the trap of making religion fit our experiences and ideals, becoming complacent and nothing but purposeless intellects like those that wasted Greece, rather than us fitting our ideals and experiences to what God has said in His scripture.

What I suggest to my free-thinking students is the *tether* approach. If you can't help but find yourself asking very difficult questions about creation, eternity and the purpose of all of this, then it is better to tie yourself to the truth before swimming out into the ocean of possibilities. Imagination is a powerful resource and talent —use it! But if you find yourself tempted by truly un-godly explanations, its best to have already in place a tether to the truth before you walk out your front door. That way you never let the sun go down on an idea that conflicts with the character of God (Jesus) or the truth of God (Bible), and thus, are always safe to ask very difficult questions even when you know you may not receive an immediate answer. It may take months, years, or decades before you learn the answer you have been seeking (perhaps never), but you will have not lost sight of what God *does* need you to know before anything else: He loves you and He is good.

Oftentimes, we are believing from understanding. Many times we are believing *to* understand. And when the Word of God reveals things I do not fully understand, I continue on, believing that the Spirit of God is faithful to teach me in due time.

iii. legends never die

"It's about being a warrior. It doesn't matter about the cost necessarily.
This is your path and you will pursue it with excellence.
You face your fear because your goal demands it.
That is the—warrior spirit."[11]

- Alex Honnold

When Marvin met Mamie Driggers, he was immediately smitten; she was, without a doubt, the prettiest and cutest woman he had ever laid eyes on. She loved the Lord, served her church, and was the kindest person in all of Florida. He knew, the second he saw her, that he needed her as his wife. The problem was that he was engaged to six other women at the same time.

Yes, Marvin was what many other men referred to as a "dandy". Always clean-cut and proper, even when working in the yard, and quite the ladies' man. But his priorities were all out of sorts. He had committed himself to six different women to wed in holy matrimony but didn't know at all if he was really looking for the right thing. He just knew he was to marry, and had no concept of how. Until he met Mamie, and it ruined everything with every prior girl.

Who is the woman that can capture the heart and attention of a legend? Only legendary people are attached to legends; otherwise, the craving and hunger for adventure will eventually separate them.

How can two walk together without agreeing where to go?[12] Mamie (or Grannie, as I knew her) was the perfect complement to Marvin. She was strong, courageous, and faithful. Nothing could stop her from hoping for better, believing for truth, and demonstrating the love of God.

Many described her as the sweetness of Marvin. While he was intense, wild and passionate, she was soft-spoken, caring, and tender. After her death, her daughter Betty would eulogize: "She was the type of woman who never condemned anyone. If someone did or said something wrong, she just point out that they didn't mean it."[13]

It was this woman that carried and trudged down highways with her children in tow to church, while her husband wasted their savings on drink and harlots. It was this woman who always prayed first and asked questions later. She was always by Marvin's side to encourage him when he failed and prop him up when he felt weak.

In the mid to late '70s, several years after Marvin passed away, Mamie went through an extremely ill period. While we know now of the Widowhood Effect and the increased probability of one dying soon after their spouse's death, this wasn't the case for Mamie. She was active and continued doing most of her daily activities despite being left alone. She remained connected to the church and tried her best to attend every opportunity; nevertheless, something was making her weak.

She couldn't keep food down, and was thinner and thinner every day, growing to small nothingness over the course of three months. At the next evening church service, she asked for her brothers and sisters to lay their hands on her and pray over whatever sickness was tormenting her. They did; together they stood on scripture.

That evening, while she hobbled herself into the shower, a place of solace and comfort, something was tickling her throat. With the water falling over her head and back, bent over double, she was hacking, trying to rend herself from the pain. Her throat was sore; her eyes and ears stung from the pressure of her violent cough; blood began to come out of the corners of her mouth, though she took no notice. Nothing could stop her; she was compelled to cough and get out whatever was hurting her.

Finally, she could feel something at the back of her mouth and the top of her throat. Her senses were non-existent at this point; her heart rate lowered from her vagal nerve agitation; she only had one purpose: to get out the thing creeping up her throat.

She reached her hand inside of her mouth and could feel something slimy and thin at the base of her tongue. After several minutes of coughing, crying, and grasping, she finally had a hold of the slippery demon that was fighting its way out of her. She began pulling slowly; she could tell the thing was fragile. She breathed every few seconds, watery blood dripping down her fingers and forearms.

After a few insufferable minutes, she dropped to the bottom of her bathtub. A bloody, slimy and dead tapeworm, several feet long was at her feet. "Thank you, Jesus…" she whispered under her breath.

From that day forward, every time someone came to visit my Grannie, they would have to witness a tapeworm, coiled inside a mason jar, on a shelf in her kitchen. It was her way of making sure she always gave glory to God for how He saved her life. What many doctors would confess as impossible, God made possible through prayer and belief.[14]

Faith never dies, though we do.[15] Our inevitable death is never the cause to stop believing and fighting. In fact, it's the legendary spirit that will continue to fight even against hopeless odds; it's in those moments that we find what we are truly capable of. But if we are not honest with our humanity and priorities on *this* side of crisis, we will never be ready to face them on the far side.

On their deathbeds, many realize, regrettably, that their focus was too often on work, success, or themselves, rather their spouse, children or legacy. We need regularly to ask ourselves what is most important, so that crisis can never misdirect our course or focus from our purpose on earth. And when death comes knocking, if we know who we are, and who our God is, we will fight with every breath to stay alive and finish giving Him glory.

iv. what we live for

"If you're going through hell, keep going."
- Winston Churchill

In 2004, the family of Enrique Álvarez and María Belón, with three sons Lucas, Simón and Tomás, was caught in a tsunami that utterly destroyed Thailand on Boxing Day, December 26th. An earthquake, measuring a magnitude of 9.2, stirred the tsunami. It caused over fifteen billion dollars in damage. The family was visiting on vacation, and though they suffered extreme loss and pain, by the grace of God, they survived the disaster.

In 2012, the family's story was portrayed on the silver screen, directed by J. A. Bayona[16]. It is one of the greatest films on survival, purpose and family that I have seen strictly for its message on what we are living for.

While the tsunami hits, María (portrayed by Naomi Watts) is separated by the rest of her family. She is tossed around under a mountain of waves and debris, injured badly, and nearly drowns. When she finally surfaces, she hears her screaming son Lucas (portrayed by Tom Holland) quickly floating away in the distance.

She haphazardly swims toward him but the two are ever-increasingly separated. Lucas screams for his mother, just in time to see a ten foot wave, full of truck tires, splintered wood and brush, come rushing at him. He dives underwater in time to be thrown around in the dark and murky ocean before a piece of debris hits him in the head and knocks him briefly unconscious. His body floats to the surface and his lungs gasp for air. His consciousness returns as he runs into a large power line and he grabs hold the concrete side of it.

"Mom!" Lucas screams. He looks around hopelessly, scared that he'll never see her again; afraid that he will never see *anyone* again. "Mom! Mom!" He begins crying, his face pressed up against the concrete pole. He composes himself long enough to look around and see his mother's body, face down, floating alongside a large pile of debris.

"Mom!" He screams one last time, hoping she is alive. She is badly bleeding, but still there. She turns her head and the two meet eyes. They both immediately push off from their foundations and swim toward one another, while being swept away in the water. María catches Lucas in her arms. He whimpers inaudibly in shock.

"We have to find some place safe," María whispers.

Lucas notices a large tree trunk down the river ahead of them, and the two decide to float toward it. They grab hold and for a brief moment have a breath and rest.

Lucas looks at his mother as she looks on the horizon in fear. "I'm scared," he whimpers.

María comes closer and comforts her son. She doesn't know if they will survive. She doesn't know what kind of damage has been done to their bodies, though they ache in pain. She doesn't know if her husband and Simón and Tomás are alive. She has no idea what to do next, though she knows she must, at all cost, keep her boy alive.

She leans close to him, as any mother would, and begins softly shushing in his ear, trying her best to calm him down and ease his fears. She whispers honestly that she is scared too, but she does so with conviction and confidence; she is a woman that is ready for what's next, refusing to surrender her life.

Lucas continues to whimper, though he is slowly composing himself more and more. "Is it over?" He asks as one that truly believes his mother has the answers and knows how to get them out of this Hell.

In life, we will inevitably go through Hell. And I use this word to describe accurately what are true trauma, desperation and fear. I used to have such a hard time with people's description of such things in life as Hell. But now I find there are few better ways to describe them. They are, in fact, the company of Hell coming into the earth and your life—here to cause you pain, grief, and agony. Those moments in our lives, where we are hopeless, are the moments of Hell, for Hell is hopeless—that is—the place without Jesus, our hope.

The root of all fruit in life is found in truth; from truth comes trust, and trust breeds commitment, and commitment accountability, and accountability results.[17] If I am to be fruitful in life, I must be accountable to some sort of commitment made on behalf of the trust found in the truth between two parties. This is how faith breeds its manifestation or fruit; it is the trust made between a person and God, founded on the truth of His goodness, and giving way to a commitment to produce results. Thus, success is found in truth. "And you will know the truth, and the truth will set you free."

Our lack of truth produces fear. As mentioned before, you are afraid of spiders, bats, and snakes because you don't understand them. People are afraid of the dark because they are afraid of the unknown. We are afraid of death because we are taught to worry about what's next. The fear of death in humans is learnt; it is unnatural because we have eternity written on our hearts.[18] If we were a people that were eternity-minded, we would never fear what's next.§§

Our lack of truth produces fear; our lack of trust produces defeat. If we were in battle, and we didn't trust the General—rather blamed Him for our casualties—we would be defeated. Regrettably, Christians and the ignorant do this regularly. If a family member dies, we blame God for wanting them more than us; if you are terminally diagnosed with cancer, you must be making God angry; if a tsunami destroys India, it's referred to as an act of God. We blame the General for our casualties, instead of recognizing He's fighting on our side!

Hebrews states that without faith it is impossible to please Him, for he who comes to God must believe that He is and that He is a rewarder of those who diligently seek Him.[19] We *must* believe, therefore our belief takes *action*. Faith, belief and trust don't just happen; therefore, if they don't just occur, that means without effort, they will dissipate. You must work to believe that He is God and that He is your rewarder because your life and the Enemy will work to dissipate that belief.

---

§§This is why, when death and eternity are taught matter-of-factly to children from parental figures, it makes sense and even births a sense of adventure.

v. in pain

"Affliction comes to us, not to make us sad but sober;
not to make us sorry but wise."
- H. G. Wells

On June 3rd, 2017, the history of man's capabilities changed forever. Alex Honnold, of Sacramento, California, free soloed the mountain face of El Capitan in Yosemite National Park. Free soloing is the sport of rock climbing without a partner or rope. It is one of the most dangerous sports and hobbies on the planet, as a climber is only a single mistake away from falling to his or her death. Most climbers consider El Capitan to be the greatest and most challenging mountain face in the world to climb; it is 3,200 feet of absolute granite. The best climbers in the world may take weeks to climb any portion of it. Alex Honnold climbed it alone, without a rope, in under four hours.

Alex has spent many interviews and presentations explaining that he did not have a death wish; he had a dream. Something inside pushed him to reach beyond the limits of his body and mind and excel at the impossible.

Alex went to extreme lengths to prove his body and mind ready to accomplish the feat. He climbed for over two-thirds of his life before seriously planning to do it. He stretched a single portion of his leg for over an entire year to make sure he could make a single grab along the difficult pitch: The Boulder Problem. He made over 3,000 perfect decisions and motions, grabbing pieces of stone less than a fingernail wide.

He reached a state of complete perfection in order to do this feat. Humans may be imperfect and will continue to trip and fall in our lives from our limitations, selfishness or ignorance; nonetheless, something about the idea of reaching complete perfection, if only for a few hours, in order to face death head-on and defeat it, is so exhilarating.

Family members and friends could not understand why he wanted to do something as dangerous and unthinkable as climbing the face of El Cap without a rope, but they at least understood that he *had* to do it. Alex clearly embodies desire demanding mastery.

There is pain in the process of perfection, and if we are going to stand before God as His perfect representative, we must start sacrificing and shedding these old dead things off. Every day, we should do something that stretches our faith, understanding, and belief. Otherwise, what was today for?

As stated, we don't hide from our pain; we use it. Everyone grows from pain. When you work out in the gym, you tone your muscles, proving them in pain. When you accomplish something worth attaining, you finish it with sweat in pain. Everyone was born —*our initial growth*—through the process of pain in our mother's childbirth. Therefore, pain develops, pain grows, and pain creates.

We can either *trust* and see results, or *mistrust* and see defeat. Trust when He says, "Cast out your nets again."

Peter replied, "We've been doing it all night."

But Jesus refused to allow Peter's exhaustion and experience deform to mistrust. "Go one more time."

It's in our discipline, effort, sweat and obedience that we find the biggest catch. And in those times, we see what we are truly made of, showing God that we are the ones He will use to shape the world.

And stand firm knowing that you are not alone; we are in this fight together. Peter, the man who learned the power of passion, encourages in his first epistle to believers that we stand firm against the devil and remain strong in our faith. "Remember that your family of believers all over the world is going through the same kind of suffering you are." This "suffering" is a derivative of *paschō*, the passion and purpose God has made us live for.

When you are weak, He is strong, and we are together.

Marvin's eyes slowly blinked open and shut. He couldn't tell where he was and briefly forgot how he even arrived. He turned his head slowly, though it hurt to do so, and he saw the mangroves hanging overhead. He heard the quiet shrill of bird-song, miles away, making him aware that his ears had indeed been ringing. He felt his mouth was hanging open, and his bottom lip was visible to him, dripping blood at irregular intervals.

A dragonfly flew across his field of vision, drawing his attention to the dash of his Willys Jeep. Now, he saw the broken cypress tree laying across the hood of his vehicle. The Jeep was dug into the mangroves, mud and tree base, its back end sticking out into the air like a strange contortionist.

He cursed under his breath and shook himself into consciousness. He reached for the stick shift and pain writhed up his entire forearm and shoulder. It felt like thousands of glass splinters running their way up his entire nervous system, across his chest, neck and down his spine. He screamed in agony and looked at his arm. The bone had fractured and was now jutting out of his forearm, just above the wrist. He cursed again and kicked the Jeep repeatedly, fighting his way through the pain.

Finally, he calmed down, breathing heavily but steadily. With his left arm, he began tearing his shirt off of himself, in long strips. Blood from the wound was all over his chest, waist and legs. After a few minutes, he had enough material to form a tourniquet and tie his arm up.

Opening the door of the Jeep, he fell into the mud. He pushed himself up from the muck and mire with his good arm and grabbed the side of the vehicle for support. He rose to his feet and looked about.

For a moment, he was completely lost. He jerked his head every which way, frantically trying to gain his bearings. A few moments passed, and he gained his bearings, remembering where he was.

Marvin planned on hunting that day and was now some eight or nine miles from the nearest piece of civilization. No one knew where he was, and it would take several days before anyone would think to look in this part of the forest.

He looked at the vehicle to see if it were at all salvageable. Three of the axles broken; only one wheel still attached to its wheel-well.

Marvin looked at the path ahead of him and cursed one last time under his breath. He prayed to God and began walking out, trying to pay as little attention to the pitter-patter off his bloody lip as he walked.

Several hours later, Marvin Alderman fell out of the woods and received proper care. His wounds were dressed and his cuts mended. But before he could be talked into going to an actual hospital, he stood from his help, hobbled on a walking stick, and trudged back into the forest. Before nightfall, Marvin came *driving* out of the woods in his Willys Jeep on only one wheel and an axle.

He consented to let someone take him to the hospital. As they drove, he laid his hand on his wrist. The bone itself was jutting out nearly two inches. He closed his eyes and prayed. By the time he and his driver arrived at the hospital, the bone had grown back into place. The blood and wound were still present, but visibly the bone had reconnected.

vi. what we die for

"A man dies when he refuses to take a stand
for that which is true."

- Martin Luther King, Jr.

In the early '40s, big game in the South was overrun with the bacterial virus anthrax. With little extensive knowledge on how to prevent and control the disease, and fear that the game population would infect much of the livestock on farms and countrysides, the government deemed necessary for all big game in Florida to be treated as a pest, and subsequently would pay citizens to hunt and kill any deer; the proof was the removed tail from a dead animal; the animal itself was to be burned.

Marvin lived to hunt. So much so that his youngest daughter Nona would confidently and publicly recite her daddy's profession as *"alligator hunter"*, much to her older sister Betty's chagrin. So when word got out that the government was willing to pay for any animal killed, and that all forms of hunting were no longer prohibited, both he and Roy jumped at the opportunity to become millionaires via deer-trade.

It was all about preparation. The two men would scour the land, searching for scars in the tree line that laid bare and open to grass and palmetto brush. They would set it ablaze with gasoline and matches, careful to contain the flames from spreading wild; the palmetto and grasslands would remain nothing but a field of black and smoldering ash. Three nights later they would return to the field in the dead of night with .22 rifles and knives strapped to their hips.

By then, deer would throng the fields, enough to make any hunter salivate. (The picture of what the animators of *Bambi* must have envisioned in their exaggerated deer-dense forests). The deer had come from every part of the wood for two reasons: to eat the newly formed sweet grass and lap up the minerals from the ash. But there were hunters in this field, stealing through the night and silently extinguishing each deer, one by one.

Marvin and Roy would spread out and move silently on the rim of the forest, intently watching each and every deer. When one wandered too far from its brothers and sisters, they would use the almost silent and perfectly accurate rifle to hit the animal in the back of the spine, immediately dropping it to its knees, removing the use of its extremities. Before the animal could bleat and alert the others, Marvin would run to its side and slice the neck with his knife. He would quickly lop the tail off of the back of the deer, stow it in his pant-leg pocket, and move on to the next animal.

In the morning, they would burn the carcasses and move on to another palmetto brush to repeat the process. Fish and Game would pay upwards of two dollars for each tail delivered. In one year, Marvin single-handedly returned over one thousand deer tails; he made the equivalent of a year's wages from killing game.

Marvin was a hunter. It was in his blood. And it's in the blood of those who want to be *legends*, because legendary actions are borne from an unsatisfied spirit, one that never waits on the game to walk up and die. You have to be resourceful, shrewd, preparatory, opportunistic and quick to strike.

These are attributes that many consider vile, equating them to those of ugly and evil dictators, sociopaths and charlatans. But that assumption is only, *and exclusively*, made by those who are living in a poverty mindset. Those that understand leadership and power know that good leaders never stop searching for great moments to attack. It's true that many evil men and women have manipulated and taken advantage of those less fortunate, using tact and shrewd behavior, but that doesn't mean it's a prerequisite for *only* vile rulers.

Every great revolutionist, the likes of Martin Luther King Jr. and Billy Graham, were mighty because of both their ability to look out for the well-being of those behind them and strike in opportunity. Imagine for a moment how our world's opportunistic leaders (from any country, diversity, or political view) would be groundbreaking if they exclusively thought of others' well-being and the advancement of the kingdom of God!

It's from the position of leadership that the Christian needs to stand; the head, and not the tail.[20] Those that think Christians should be weak and submissive are the foolish ones complaining about getting walked all over. Jesus was humble, but he never let someone step on His neck (unless He wanted them to[21]).

It's in the hunter mindset that we find the thing necessary for *legends*. The person who is willing to put their life, time, energy, and preparation on the line for a simple meal. In a very metaphorical sense, too many of us think the meal should be waiting at the supermarket aisle, already dead and packaged. Legends bring the animal to the supermarket for others to feast.

Of course, all of this is quite *metaphorical*. I'm not suggesting we all start hunting our own hamburger. But I am suggesting we become hunters of greatness and success. We must hunt for the kingdom of God to advance.

In the '50s, Marvin was a minister again, preaching in Palm Bay, FL. He had a long drive every Sunday morning to his church before Mamie would bring the teenage kids to service later in the day. On his way, Marvin would pass by Jim, a member of the community whose wife Lisa was attending the service regularly, but couldn't seem to get him to attend.

Jim always had an excuse and desire to be somewhere else. He didn't awfully despise the church or what it stood for; he just couldn't understand the value of corporate religion. He appreciated what Marvin and his family would do for the community. Jim just didn't have time for that church thing; he had his ice business to manage and a family to provide for.

Sunday morning, Marvin was driving along Palm Bay Road when he saw Jim sweating and swearing in front of his ice-truck in his front yard. A plume of steam and smoke lifted up from the hood of the truck.

Marvin looked down at his watch. Service would start in about 90 minutes. He pulled into Jim's driveway and walked up to him. He was wearing his Sunday best like he always did; a white dress shirt, black slacks, and a bolo tie (he had swapped out the bowtie today).

"Morning, Jim." Marvin greeted with a smile.

"Christ," Jim mumbled under his breath. "Uh—hey Reverend. Can't come to Mass today…" He motioned to the broken-down truck in front of him. "I gotta get the truck running for tomorrow."

Marvin looked at the truck in front of him. He pursed his lips and breathed deeply. Then he unhinged his long sleeves and rolled them up around his forearms. "Gimme a wrench."

Two hours later, the hood slammed shut, and the truck kicked over. Marvin rolled his sleeves down, shook the hand of Jim and said confidently, "I'll see you at church." Jim never missed another Sunday service with his wife again.

Jesus said, *"I am sending you out as sheep among wolves. So be as shrewd as snakes and harmless as doves."*[22] Too many of us either act like doves getting eaten by snakes, or a snake that forgot what he's hunting for. What Jesus is insinuating, is that we need to search and be ready to strike at opportunity—face our fears, overcome our pain, and in the process, build relationships and bridges with God's children. Our strike is as harmless as a dove; it is gentle and covered in grace and love. Strike sure. Strike often. For every opportunity, especially that which requires the most pain and sacrifice, carries legacy.

vii. what will you die for?

"For a person who is dying only eternity counts."
- Friedrich Durrenmatt

The Boxing Day tsunami has hit India's beachside; María Belón and her son Lucas are separated from the rest of their family. They do not know if their family members are alive or where they should go; they only know that they must keep moving in order to survive. Lucas' mother is severely injured. Her calf has been ripped to shreds, her body is bruised and bleeding, she can barely walk without her son's assistance, and she has ingested pounds of dirty water into her stomach.

As they walk through heaping piles of dangerous debris, muck and water, they find a large tree that could give them safety and protection from waves, wildlife, and bacteria. While on their way, they hear the sound of a small boy crying out for help, far in the distance.

"Wait, did you hear that?" María slows her walk, looking every which way, trying to find where the direction of the voice has come from.

Lucas is nearly unresponsive, keeping his head down and his eyes forward. "Mom, there's nothing we can do."

María stops him. "Wait," she whispers, with a motherly gaze. She tries to get Lucas to help her look.

"We are almost there." Lucas persists. "We have to get to safety."

"We have to help that boy." She is no longer listening to Lucas.

"Mom, if another wave catches us down here, we will die." Lucas tries to grab her attention again. "We have to climb that tree —right now!"

The little boy cries from the distance again. "Where are you?!" María shouts into the unknown.

"Mom, look at you! We need help. We can't risk it, Mom. Come on!"

María attempts to make Lucas understand, knowing full well that she can't help the lost boy without the assistance of her son. "Listen —what if that boy was Simón or Tomás? What if they needed help? You'd want someone to help them, wouldn't you—"

"Simón and Tomás are dead!" Lucas bows his head. He begins crying from the weight that has been placed on his shoulders and the hopelessness in his heart. His mother bows down to meet his eyes. She whispers in his ear, *"Even if it's the last thing we do..."*

Who can give it all and then go one more time?

These are the people God will shape the earth into Heaven with because they do not believe in survival but in purpose. No matter the cost, even if it's the last thing we do, we will continue fighting for God's children to know He loves them.

And about the ninth hour, Jesus cried with a loud voice, saying, "Eli, Eli, lama sabachthani?" that is to say, "My God, my God, why hast thou forsaken me?"[23] His' finals words hung in the sky for a moment, as every man, woman and child, Roman soldier, Jew and Gentile felt the magnitude of such a statement. They saw Him bow his head, whisper *its* finality, and give up His body. An earthquake shook the ground, lightning cracked the sky, the temple crumbled to pieces, the veil of God ripped to shreds, and out of the gravesite men and women of centuries past dug themselves from the ground and began walking through the City of Jerusalem.[24]

I was taught many times in my upbringing that this was the moment that Jesus took all the sin of the world upon Himself and God looked away, forsaking Him and letting Him die***, becoming sin for us all.[25] But I don't believe this any longer.

The truth is in the Word of God. While studying, my father came across two pieces of scripture in Isaiah 41:17, *"the poor and needy search for water, but there is none; their tongues are parched with thirst. But I the Lord will answer them; I, the God of Israel, will not forsake them."* and Psalm 22:24, *"For He has not despised nor abhorred the affliction of the afflicted; Nor has He hidden His face from Him; But when He cried to Him, He heard."*

God the Father does not look away from the afflicted, nor did He look away from Jesus' affliction. *Sabachthani* is found in the root word *Shebaq*, meaning *"to leave, forsake"*. God does not "hide His face" or *Cathar*, *"concealing oneself"*. He does not turn His eyes ever; He did not look away from Jesus in His death.

When Jesus was at His lowest; defeated on the Cross, dying, mocked, scourged, and left for dead, even then, He knew that God didn't forsake Him. But *we* did. As Jesus uttered His final words, He looked up to heaven and called upon His Father's name one final time on earth, "My God, my God," and then looking down upon His creation, He looked at every Jew, Gentile, and betrayer and said to us, "Why have *you*, *Israel*, left me?"

When life gets impossibly hard, and the journey becomes unbearable, are you going to throw your head up and *abandon all hope*? Or are you going to remind yourself of the purpose again? Jesus never once gave up. He, again and again, reminded Himself,

---

***I've also heard perverted theologians postulate that Jesus gave up on God at this moment—this would be a perfect example of letting philosophy create our own demonic religion.

amidst frustration, betrayal, torment and exhaustion, of what He was doing and why He was doing it.

At the moment He uttered His final words, He died for the purpose.

What will you die for? *Who* will you die for?

Even if it's the last thing you do, are you willing to go save one more?

1954.

The sun is out, beating on the barren dirt highway in Palm Bay, Florida. Marvin drives quietly down the road behind a large blue pickup truck. He looks to his right and sees swampland and marsh as far as the eye can see; a Sandhill Crane stands still in the hunt; six green sliders topple and splash into the water; an eight-foot alligator rests on the edge of its kingdom.

A crow flies across the front of Marvin's pickup and brings his attention back to the road ahead of him. He sees far in the distance a black man cleaning up his lunch from the bed of his pickup. And then time slows down. The blue truck in front of Marvin speeds up. It throws dust into the air. Marvin squints his eyes from the cloud overrunning his open window; he turns the crank over as quickly as he can to shield himself.

He focuses his eyes forward again and sees the blue truck has suddenly stopped alongside the highway. White smoke is lifting into the air on the far side; he realizes there has been an accident. His foot lifts from the accelerator. Strangely, the blue truck is backing up, and before he can see what happened, it has sped away, throwing dirt, rocks and smoke everywhere.

All that is left is the broken and tattered tail end of the black man's truck, the man holding onto the edge of his tailgate and his life; he falls down into the dirt. Marvin quickly realizes that this was not an accident. The driver has purposely crashed into and attempted murder of the black man eating his lunch.

Marvin stops his truck and runs from it, leaving the door open and engine running. As he approaches the man on the ground, he sees how dreadful it is. Both legs have been severed from the man at the knees. He is screaming and writhing in pain, coughing blood and throwing it all over the side of his vehicle from his stubbed legs.

Marvin clenches his jaw and kneels down beside the man. He attempts to calm the man down, but he is flailing everywhere. Blood is spurting at an irreparable rate out of the man's arteries. Marvin puts his weight on the man and reaches into each leg, grabbing hold of his arteries in each fist; both men are covered in blood and sweat. The man continues to scream in shock and disbelief.

"Brother!" Marvin yells. The man finally stops shouting, though his eyes are shut, and he is quietly begging to die.

"Brother, do you know Jesus?" The man opens his eyes and looks at Marvin. He sees a little white man in a suit and bowtie staring back at him. "—because you're about to meet Him." The little man's hands are inside of his legs and both he and the little white man are covered in blood. The man shakes his head back at Marvin.

At that moment, Marvin prays and asks the man to pray with him. He leads him into Jesus' salvation and at that, the man dies in Marvin's arms. He holds him for a few minutes before he lets his body go.

We must know what we are fighting for. The attributes of legends are the ones that will shape the world. We are opportunistic, powerful, shrewd visionaries, and with that power comes a sobering reality. We will change the world. And if we don't know what we are fighting for, we will destroy it.

I pray to God that when crisis hits, I respond like my great-grandfather and run to the hurting, instead of after the offender. It's the messier, uglier, and oftentimes sadder job; it's the one that sometimes feels less impactful. Nevertheless, it's the one that Jesus would have run after.

Jesus stood before his followers and naysayers and told a story about a man who was attacked and left for dead along the road. A priest and Levite came along and avoided him altogether, passing along the other side. Then a despised Samaritan[26] came along, and when he saw the man, he felt compassion for him. Going over to him, the Samaritan soothed his wounds with olive oil and wine and bandaged them. Then he put the man on his own donkey and took him to an inn where he took care of him. The next day he handed the innkeeper two silver coins, telling him, "Take care of this man. If his bill runs higher than this, I'll pay you the next time I'm here."

After telling the story, Jesus asked everyone, "Now which of these three would you say was a neighbor to the man who was attacked by bandits?"

"The one who showed him mercy," they all replied.

The world can look like a terrible pain-ridden place because no one ever talks about the man who goes to save his brother alongside the road; we only ever talk about the man who hit him and sped away. It's by society's cruel design that only the one screaming the loudest is often heard in media, politics, or around the water-cooler. And Christians tend to get a bad reputation because a certain group of them may be out in front displaying acts of judgment and foolishness.

If we don't know what we are fighting for, we can get in over our heads and display the wrong side of Christ's heart. Does Christ get angry? Absolutely. But does his anger ever outweigh his mercy? Never.

It's not flashy to be quiet when others are screaming. It's not easy to help the hurting when we are full of rage brought upon us by the acts of evil. But too many Christians are known by what they're against; we need to be known by what we are for.

How did Jesus respond to acts of cruelty, racism and prejudice? He often ignored the offenders and helped the hurting.[27] He cared about making sure those that hurt, knew He loved them.[28] And he barely gave any time to those who were throwing barbaric criticism at Him and His followers.[29]

It was nearly time for the Jewish Passover celebration,[30] so Jesus went to Jerusalem. In the Temple area, He saw merchants selling cattle, sheep and doves for sacrifices; He also saw dealers at tables exchanging foreign money. Jesus made a whip from some ropes and chased them all out of the Temple. He drove out the sheep and cattle, scattered the money changers' coins over the floor, and turned over their tables. Then, going over to the people who sold doves, He told them, "Get these things out of here. Stop turning my Father's house into a marketplace!"

Many things may make Jesus sad—our hatred, racism, prejudices, ignorance, sin—but only one thing makes Him *angry:* The misrepresentation of God and making people pay their way into Heaven. It's Jesus' character of loving all of God's children and having them in Heaven with Him at all cost (*His cost*), that He portrays to us.

The act of stopping someone from being ignorant or hateful (chasing the offender) only fixes a problem for a day, but salvation fixes an eternity. Jesus Himself didn't run after all those that accused the woman caught in adultery.[31] He didn't follow them home and teach them some long lesson on why they were wrong for being judgmental and murderous. Instead, He knelt down and helped the woman to her feet.

Chasing the offender, hatred, or screaming madmen will only fill us with the identity of Judge. Chase the hurting, needful and abandoned. Help them and you will create history—that is what we die for.

Many believe that Time moves at a constant speed, and age is subject to that speed and length. But Time is not a constant; it is a construct. A fabled idea to make sense out of death and sin. I postulate that Time itself began when Adam and Eve first sinned because at that moment, death entered the world.

Imagine for a moment, your life without death, regret, hurt, pain, exhaustion, or hunger. You would have no need to fear what may come, nor any painful memory of what had. You would be free from a life of needing to rest or restore because your life would be a continual state of joy and freedom. Eternity would be an obvious truth because death would never be a marker out in front of you on some arbitrary date.

You and I were made eternal. And Time, the damnable thing that it is, results from sin. It's not truly a *real* thing; it's only one that we have made up to explain why we fear "an end", why we have moments of hurts, and why we demand rest when we are tired.

This is why you find yourself saying, "It feels like Tuesday" when it is actually Friday, and why it feels like eleven o'clock when it's only eight! The spinning of our planet around the sun cannot determine your process, or amount of guilt, struggle, or weight that pushes you down; only your life can do that. We will all die physically, but we were all made to live eternally.

When Marvin turned the corner around our sun for the sixty-sixth time in 1970, he had borne enough for two lifetimes, so much so that his body couldn't bear to hang on much longer. He fought through decades of guilt and hating himself for what he put his wife and children through, as well as the fear that he never did enough to make God proud. And while he was only 66, it was enough to cap his lifetime here on earth. What doctors didn't understand then to be Alzheimer's now, they diagnosed Marvin with the "hardening of the arteries".

In his last few months on earth, his children admitted him to an assisted living facility to help him with his ever-increasing loss of the surrounding reality. And though he was losing his memories every day of who people were around him, and all of the wonderful legends and tall tales that he had experienced, he never lost sight of who God was and what his mission was here on earth.

Every day, Marvin was walking up and down the halls of the assisted living facility with a Bible in his hand and a prayer on his lips. He would stop in each room of his fellow tenants and minister the Gospel to them with the Word, prayer, and the laying on of the hands.

One afternoon, Betty and Mamie walked into his room, only to find a despondent Marvin sitting in his favorite recliner in the corner. Unfortunately, it had been a week since the two ladies were able to see him. Mamie had slipped and fallen, twisting her ankle a few days before. Though she was fine, her leg had swollen up, and it hurt her to walk.

They sat beside a dazed Marvin, confused by the presence of these two strange women in his room. He balked at them, growing frustrated and angry. Part of him understood that he should know these women, but his brain couldn't fire properly, and the memories wouldn't connect. After a few moments of awkward silence, Betty began playing a recording of some of Marvin's favorite hymns.

EVEN IF IT'S THE LAST THING WE DO

Lord, haste the day when my faith shall be sight,
The clouds be rolled back as a scroll;
The trump shall resound, and the Lord shall descend,
It is well with my soul.

The glaze over Marvin's eyes dissolved, he closed them shut, and his lips began to move. Betty smiled as her father returned and began to sing aloud. Tears were slowly trickling down his cheeks. With eyes shut, he reached and took the hand of Mamie. She put her other hand on top of his; they both held each other in silence, crying both from joy and loss.

When Marvin opened his eyes again, he was *back*. He looked at Betty the way he always looked at his princess—with pride and admiration. He turned his head and looked Mamie in the eyes. She was his fortress; his queen; his reason and support who never left his side.

He spoke slowly and in broken sentences, but the three carried on for some time, talking and enjoying one another's presence. At some point in the conversation, he remembered that his bride walked in on a hobbled foot. He looked down at the swollen purple ankle.

He dropped to his knees and put his hands on Mamie's leg. "In the name of Jesus, swelling, *go away*." As he let go, the swelling of Mamie's leg faded and disappeared right before Betty's eyes. The coloration of her leg returned to normal. Mamie stood and no longer had pain.

Weeks and months disappeared; Marvin continued to walk the halls and share the Good News of Jesus Christ. Every visit from Mamie included praise and worship music to bring his memories back. They spent their last moments holding hands and ministering the Gospel, in the little time they had, around a small living facility in Ruskin, Florida. His body gave up, and his spirit went to Heaven, June 11th, 1970, only four months after being admitted to hospice care. He fought for his King until the end.

viii. make peace with God

Once you find yourself no longer failing, you have failed to move forward, dream bigger and try harder. There is a holiness that occurs in the falling. In the 2005 film *Batman Begins*[32], Alfred Pennyworth educates the broken and defeated Bruce Wayne, *"Why do we fall?—So that we can learn to pick ourselves back up."* If you are to live a life like King David, Peter, and Abraham—a life that is Legendary—you will have to learn to pick yourself back up.

Sometimes failing in life doesn't even look like sin. It has a name like depression, fear, doubt, defeat, betrayal, or abandonment. You don't have to do something wrong in order to fail. Sometimes life just smacks you in the face.

People will accuse you of something you didn't do, challenging your integrity and character. People will trash your ideals to your face; your closest brothers demoralizing everything you live for. But those things are not your destiny. They are those that will propel you *toward* it. A life worth living will be full of patience, faith and failure.

You weren't born to endure, but designed to learn how. A baby endures nothing; it cries about everything and demands satisfaction *now*. You were designed to learn endurance because leadership is built on the back of it. If you want to succeed, thrive, and do *anything* legendary in this life, you will have to learn to suffer long. The very reason being that when others suffer, you know how to provide relief.

"The Holy Spirit produces this kind of fruit in our lives:
love, joy, peace, [the ability to suffer long], *kindness, goodness,*
faithfulness, gentleness and self-control."

Galatians 5:22-23

After Jesus' death and resurrection, Peter found himself in a bit of existential crisis.[33] He followed his Savior and Lord until Jesus needed him most, and then he abandoned Him in cowardice. He left the Messiah to fend for Himself; more importantly, he left his *friend* to die alone.

But now the Messiah had returned. He was back, blinking in and out of different gardens and living rooms, showing people that He had defeated death. But something was still off between the two friends; they hadn't spoken about *that moment* yet, and Peter didn't know deep down what his purpose was now. What was he to do? Had he missed his opportunity? When Jesus needed him most, he gave up.

"I'm going fishing." Peter decided one evening. Perhaps Peter was giving up, or perhaps he was just trying to go back to where it all began with him and Jesus. This was the thing indeed that he was doing when he first heard God call him.

We'll come too," Thomas replied, motioning toward Nathanael, James, John and two others in the room. So they went out in the boat. They fished all night, and all night it felt like that same miserable evening that they first met Jesus face to face. The fish weren't running, and it only made the whole night all the more painful.

At dawn the men made their way back into shore and saw a figure standing on the bank; they couldn't quite make out who it was, yet.

"Fellows," the figure cried out. "Have you caught any fish?"

Nathanael, who was the least miserable, cried out, "No, it's been a shod of a night!"

"Throw your net on the right-hand side of the boat, and you'll get some!"

The men looked at each other in silence. There was a bit of unspoken anticipation in their work, an uneasiness of trepidation and excitement. The men threw the nets on the other side of the boat, and to their amazement and satisfaction, it worked like it had years before. They could not haul in the net because there were so many fish in it.

John turned to Peter in wonder and disbelief. "It's the *Lord*!" His voice was broken and came out just above a whisper.

At this, Peter looked about him and quickly grabbed his tunic; the tunic that he wore in his ministry, yet had since left behind in order to fish with his comrades. He put it back on and jumped feet first, awkwardly and like a child, into the sea. He came up for air and began turning arm over arm, paddling himself to shore.

I believe Jesus was recreating this moment Peter, Nathanael, Thomas, James, John and the others we do not know the names of (must have slipped John's memory), in order to give them purpose again. All of these men remembered it as the moment they were first given hope and trust.

Jesus is telling all of us: "Don't give up throwing the nets out, just because it gets hard. Not even because I die in the process. There is a task at hand, and we will continue working until it is complete."

Peter's metaphorical response with the taking of his tunic is powerful and genuine. He was dressed for the wrong job. Too often when we face tragedy or pain, we go back to our previous occupation—the occupation of garden-tender[34] rather than fisher-of-men. We start providing for ourselves again. But we aren't meant to provide for ourselves; we are meant to provide for God's children. There are more fish to be had. That's what makes a legend worth telling; that's what makes you a *legend*.

The truth will set the world free, now take it to them, even if it's the last thing you do. Jesus doesn't need *Babies*, and He's not looking to walk with *Adults*. He needs *Parents*—those willing to work to feed others. When life is so hard, you feel you are up there with your arms outstretched and all the world has left you—in that moment—know that He never left you, never forsook you, even if it's the last thing you did.

Go throw the net out again. "We worked all night." Go out one more time!

ix. legend

Spring was here; the sun shone down on the back of the five figures' necks. The oldest and foremost of the group was tired but purposeful; he was hunting for the name amidst the hundreds and thousands of metal plates. It was here somewhere. The tall blades of grass bent and crushed beneath his footsteps. The cackle of cicadas sung in the distance at a numbing volume. Sweat dripped down from his brow and his son sitting on his shoulders pulled at his hair and complained about his desire to get down and run around.

"Where is it, Daddy?" AnnaBelle asked me as she playfully danced about behind, in a broken line led by myself with Harvey on my shoulders, her sister Sydney beside her, and Carlia some twenty paces behind looking eagerly about the headstones for that special name. We made our way to a partitioned area of the cemetery that was reserved for ministers and spouses. In the center of all of it was a single proud word: *Alderman*.

When we found Marvin and Mamie's headstone, it proudly said the words: MAKE PEACE WITH GOD AND MEET US IN HEAVEN. I know that these were the words of a man that gave everything for his Father in Heaven, but was tormented by the idea that he hadn't given enough, sacrificed enough, or loved enough to make sure those closest to him were saved.

His oldest son Lewis never truly came back to the faith after being removed from seminary; his youngest Nona was the wild child who, as long as *he* knew, was lost.[†††] His heart grieved until the end that, though he may have saved thousands, he may have failed at the most important. But that's what much of life is—the walking through time and space filled with regret, pain and sin. We have a mission and we have a calling to be legends. All we are meant to do is love and trust our Father and love and serve His children.

Marvin didn't know what would happen to his children, but I do. I live knowing there are countless believers and ministers that followed this man's vision and example in our family. And now I finally know what the meaning of his headstone truly is. We aren't meant to just *make peace with God* but meant to *create* peace *alongside* Him, until the day we die. This is what Marvin lived by.

Marvin was a quiet, humble, wild, proud man who had the longest alligator in his home and the tallest corn in his crops. Everywhere he went, his Bible went too. He believed God's faithfulness to save, heal and raise the dead. He lived every ounce making sure God knew *he loved Him* and making sure others knew *He loved them.*

He did these things because he believed faithfully, loved passionately, regretted deeply, and consequently changed the world

---

[†††] Nona received Jesus' salvation later in life after Marvin had passed away.

forever. Not because he wanted to go down in history as a legend, but because his legend was to make peace with God.

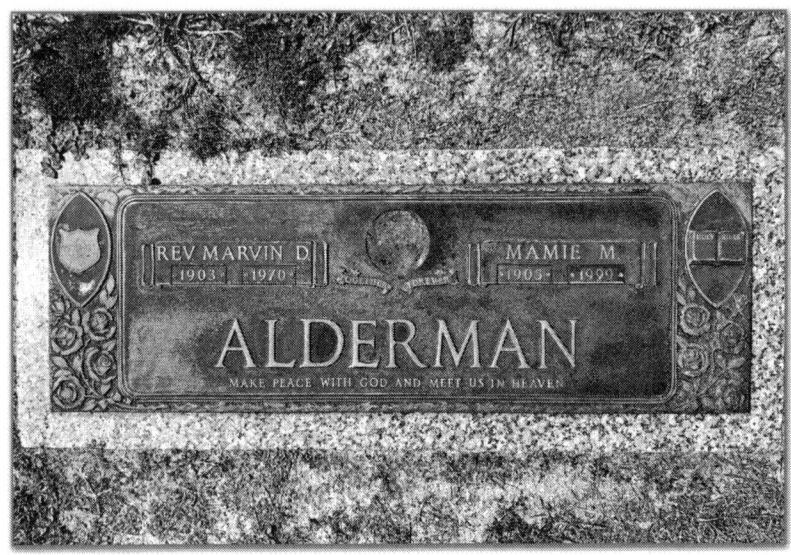

"Make Peace with God and Meet Us in Heaven."

At Marvin's, Mamie's, and Leland's gravesite with my children.
Palm Bay, FL - Spring, 2019

Gene and Betty Coulter with Keith and Carlia Alderman
"Thanks for all the fact checking and love, Aunt Betty."
Spring, 2019

From left to right: Mamie, Lewis, Betty, Leland, Nona, Marvin. 1946. Miami.

NOTES:

Part 1: DESIRING LEGENDS

1. Mark 4:34-40
2. Mark 5:1-20
3. Matthew 9:9; John 1:43; Mark 1:17
4. Luke 18:22-23; Luke 9:57-62
5. Mark 5:19-21
6. Mark 7:31
7. Mark 8
8. Gibson, Mel, director. Braveheart. Icon Entertainment International, 1995.
9. 2 Timothy 1:7
10. 2 Samuel 11:2-5
11. 2 Samuel 11:14-17
12. Romans 8:31
13. Revelation 12:11
14. Mark 5:22-43

Part 2: EARNING LEGENDS

1. Matthew 26:39, 40
2. Luke 22:43
3. Romans 5:8
4. Lamentations 3:22, 23
5. Luke 22:44
6. Matthew 5:48; 1 Timothy 3:4
7. Matthew 19:26
8. Matthew 9:12
9. John 2:15
10. 2 Timothy 2:14
11. Matthew 14:29
12. Joshua 2:4
13. Acts 14:19, 20

NOTES

14. Matthew 14:28-33
15. Luke 22:54-57

Part 3: LEGEND CHARACTER

1. Genesis 22
2. 1 Corinthians 2:9
3. Hudson, Russ, and Brian Taylor. "How The System Works." The Enneagram Institute, 2017, www.enneagraminstitute.com/how-the-enneagram-system-works.
4. Matthew 19:26
5. "Passion." Merriam-Webster, Merriam-Webster, www.merriam-webster.com/dictionary/passion.
6. "G3958 - paschō - Strong's Greek Lexicon (KJV)." Blue Letter Bible. Web. 2 Aug, 2019. <https://www.blueletterbible.org//lang/lexicon/lexicon.cfm?Strongs=G3958&t=KJV>.
7. Acts 1:3
8. 2 Corinthians 1:3, 4
9. 1 John 2:2
10. John 2:15
11. Romans 10:13
12. James 1:2-3
13. Hebrews 11
14. Nehemiah 1-8:10
15. Lamentations 3
16. Hebrews 13:8
17. Isaiah 43:19
18. Exodus 14:14
19. Nehemiah 8:10
20. Romans 5:8
21. Philippians 4:6
22. Gibson, E. J., & Walk, R. D. (1960). The "visual cliff." Scientific American, 202, 67–71
23. Lewis, C. S. Perelandra. Scribner, 2003.

24. Lieber, Jeffrey, et al. "Lost/What They Died For."
    Season 6, episode 16.
25. Lewis, C. S. The Voyage of the Dawn Treader. HarperCollins
    Children's Books, 2001.

Part 4: NO ONE CAN STEAL YOUR DESTINY

1. James 4:14
2. Genesis 37:5-11
3. Genesis 37:28; Genesis 39:20
4. Genesis 41:16
5. Judges 13:5
6. Judges 14:18, 19
7. Judges 16:4, 5
8. Judges 14:19; Judges 15:14; Judges 16:17; Judges 16:20
9. Judges 16:28-30
10. Romans 3:23
11. Romans 6:23
12. Ephesians 4:32
13. Romans 12:2
14. Ephesians 4:22-24
15. Matthew 18:15-17
16. Acts 15:36-39
17. Galatians 2:11
18. Philemon 24
19. 2 Peter 3:15
20. Psalm 7:11
21. 1 Samuel 16:7
22. Matthew 7:15, 20
23. Matthew 7:1, 2
24. 1 Corinthians 12:4
25. 1 Corinthians 12:11
26. Mark 9:33, 34; Mark 10:35-37; Luke 22:24
27. Hebrews 12:1
28. Esther 4:14

NOTES

29. Romans 10:9
30. 1 Corinthians 12:5, 6
31. Luke 22:26

Part 5: EVEN IF IT'S THE LAST THING WE DO
1. Nolan, Christopher, director. Batman Begins. Warner Bros., 2005.
2. 1 Corinthians 3:1-3
3. Hebrews 5:13, 14
4. Hebrews 6:1-3
5. 1 Corinthians 4:14-16
6. 1 Corinthians 8:13
7. Jwxr, director. YouTube. YouTube, YouTube, 16 May 2018, www.youtube.com/watch?v=DdvN4WqJh6g.
8. John 8:31, 32
9. 1 Corinthians 2:14
10. Lewis, C. S. The Weight of Glory and Other Addresses. HarperOne, 2001.
11. Chin, Jimmy and Elizabeth Chai Vasarhelyi, directors. Free Solo. Itinerant Films, 2018.
12. Amos 3:3
13. Simpson, Lee. "'Granny' Alderman Dies at 93." Florida Today, 1999.
14. Mark 9:29
15. Hebrews 11:13
16. Bayona, J. A., director. The Impossible. Mediaset Espana, Summit Entertainment, 2012.
17. Lencioni, Patrick, and Charles Stransky. The Five Dysfunctions of a Team. Random House, Inc, 2002.
18. Ecclesiastes 3:11
19. Hebrews 11:6
20. Deuteronomy 28:13
21. John 19:10, 11
22. Matthew 10:16
23. Mark 15:34

24. Matthew 27:50-52
25. 2 Corinthians 5:21
26. Luke 10:25-37
27. John 8:6
28. Luke 5:13; Matthew 9:6
29. Matthew 15:12, 13
30. John 2:13-16
31. John 8:9, 10
32. Nolan, Christopher, director. Batman Begins. Warner Bros., 2005.
33. John 21:1-7
34. Genesis 2:15

APPENDIX A:
Furthering Tall Tales

There are a few remarkable albeit ridiculous other tales about Marvin that couldn't seem to find their way into my overarching theme, nevertheless they were too special to leave unshared.

I never met Marvin, therefore I often find myself picturing a lumbering powerful handsome Mr. Universe and forget that he was only five-foot-six and barely ever over a buck-fifty in weight. His stockiness and determination were otherworldly though.

He was quite the jack-of-all-trades, doing his best to master different techniques and abilities. He and his seven siblings grew up in an agricultural family working cattle and orange groves for their main income. He and his brothers were perfectionists when it came to firearms. They weren't highly educated, so they hunted ccaselessly, becoming regular crack-shots with rifles and pistols, to make up for the lost time.

For whatever reason Roy and Marvin taught themselves the oddest abilities. Marvin had the ability to pump his legs so fast that he could walk across a lake without sinking into it. His greatest attempt at this was when he crossed a pond while holding a newspaper open and reading it, and never sinking below the waist.

His physical prowess never ended. He and Roy taught themselves how to walk on their hands so well, Marvin could step up onto a chair and drink from a glass of water *all the while on his hands!* He and Roy also had an odd fancy for performing backflips, commonly as means to impress and/or celebrate. Every birthday until each turned *fifty*, they would perform a perfect backflip.

APPENDIX B:
"Marvin Daniel Alderman" Timeline

Joseph "Doll" Alderman (1879-1968)
Baptist Minister
Jennie Alderman (1881-1945)
Children:
- Dora (1901)
- Clarence (1902)
- **Marvin Daniel**, born 1903; died 1970 from "hardening of the arteries" (Alzheimer's); Church of God Minister
- Vury (1905)
- Roy (1908)
- Adeline (1910)
- Ida Mae (1914)
- Iris (1919)

Marvin and Mamie Driggers were married December 20, 1924 in Highlands, FL
Children:
- Charles Lewis: Feb 4, 1928 - April 23, 1998 — Died at the age of seventy; He was kicked out of seminary in 1946 at the age of eighteen. Marvin left the Church immediately.
- **Leland Leroy**: August 6, 1935 - Aug 26, 2002 — Died at the age of sixty-seven from Alzheimer's; Church of God Minister; He

was ten years old when Lewis was kicked out of seminary;
seventeen when Marvin repents
Leland marries Faye Mewbourn in April 1961 in Palm Beach, FL.
Children:
- **John Marvin**‡‡‡ - April 20, 1962
- Vanessa - 1963, deceased 7 months and 10 days later
- Maranatha - December 23, 1964
- Desiree - February 25, 1966
- Betty - November 3, 1937 - currently living in Palm Bay, FL.
She and her husband Gene of sixty years, still attend the same
Church of God that Marvin pastored and married the couple in
1959. She was eight years old when Lewis was kicked out of
seminary; fifteen when Marvin repented
- Nona - December 13, 1940 - Aug 13, 1989 —Died at the age of
forty-eight from Lupus; She was five years old when Lewis
was kicked out of seminary; twelve when Marvin repented.
Buried in Melbourne, FL

1924. Marvin and Mamie are married
1924. Marvin goes to Frostproof and is anointed. He preaches. Many are
saved and called to the Church of God ministry.
1945. Marvin is recognized by University of Miami's theologians
1946. Lewis is expelled from Church of God Bible Training
1953. Summer Camp Meeting, Marvin repents
1953. Marvin begins pastoring again
1955. Marvin begins pastoring Church of God Palm Bay, continuing for
the next 15 years
1970. Marvin is admitted to a mental health assisted living facility in
Ruskin, FL, diagnosed with "hardening of the arteries"
1970. Summer, Marvin dies from Alzheimer's

Marvin Daniel Alderman died on June 11, 1970 in Ruskin, Florida at the
age of sixty-six. He is buried in Palm Bay
Mamie "Grannie" Alderman died on April 22, 1999 in Melbourne at the
age of ninety-four. She is buried in Palm Bay

---

‡‡‡ author's patriarchal lineage is **accented**

APPENDIX C:
Granddaddy's First Deer

The following is from a handwritten note Leland wrote after bagging his first deer alongside his daddy Marvin, the winter of 1953.

My First Deer

"It was the twenty-fourth of December, 1953, and the day was hot and sweltering. But this was hunting season and even though Daddy and I had walked 5 miles into camp the day before, slogging through mud, stumbling over rocks, bumping against cypress knees and carrying our bedding and hunting equipment on our backs; we were ready to go that morning because we were hunting in the Florida Everglades and we knew that the deer were there. (There were 6 men already in camp!—the other men in our party were already in earlier.)

We got up and cooked breakfast early that morning and were ready to head out hunting by seven o'clock. We divided into two parties: five men went West and Steve Roberts, Daddy, me and Steve's dog headed East.

We struck trail of a young buck and two does outside of camp about 300 yards and followed them Southeast until about nine o'clock and finally jumped them in a cypress head but both Daddy and I missed our shots. Daddy didn't have a good open shot and I gave him too much lead.

We headed back up a Northeasterly direction to get back on our original course and never struck another trail until about eleven. It was a bad direction; we followed it until dinner time and then stopped for a rest. We made coffee and ate some Vienna sausage sandwiches and some oranges which we had brought along as something to keep us going.

We then picked up the trail again and it took a winding, zig-zag direction East. The trail we were following was getting fresher all the time. About 2 o'clock, we came to a big Palmetto island with several big cypress heads in it. Daddy flanked on the West and I was East of Steve and the dog. We slowly headed North, upwind, into the Palmettos and in a few minutes Steve fired and shouted at me. I turned and looked and there was the deer about 40 yards away taking flying leaps. He really looked like a great monarch with those big antlers held erect and his white tail sticking up and waving like a flag in a frightened, defiant sort of way.

I raise my 12 gauge double-barrel shotgun to my shoulder and took careful aim and fired twice but the deer ran on.

Steve told me, 'Son, if you can't do any better than that you'll never kill a deer.' Then I told him that when I shot I saw the deer's tail fall even though he ran on. So we went over where the deer had run and we saw blood and foam on the Palmettos. So I had hit him after all.

The dog picked up the trail and we followed it for about a quarter of a mile, and there the deer lay, and he was a big one. He was a 10 point buck—a real 'gran' daddy', and I had killed him using no. 4 buck shot and only hit him with one pellet.

He weighed about 190 pounds field dressed, but we were carrying him back to camp, and camp was four miles away, so he became pretty heavy. He dressed out 155 pounds of the best venison in the whole world and next day it made the best Christmas dinner I ever ate. "

- Leland Alderman

My First Deer.

i. It was ~~a fact~~ ~~the~~ twenty-fourth of December 1953 and the day was hot and sweltering. This was hunting season and even though Daddy and I had walked 5 miles into camp the day before, slogging through mud, stumbling over rocks, bumping against cypress knees and carrying our bedding and hunting equipment on our backs, ~~we~~ were ready to go ~~that~~ morning because we were hunting in the Florida Everglades and we ~~knew~~ that the deer were there. (There were 6 men already in camp.') ⑺⓪ (The other men in our party were already in camp.)

We got up and cooked breakfast that morning and were ready to head out by seven o'clock. We divided into two parties: ~~four~~ five men went west and Steve Roberts, Daddy, me, and Steve's dog headed East. ③⓪

~~We followed the dog until about nine o'clock.~~

We struck trail of a young buck and two does outside of camp about 300 yards, and followed them SouthEast until about nine o'clock and finally jumped them in a cypress head but both Daddy and I missed our shots. Daddy didn't have ~~good~~ very ~~shot~~ and I ~~didn't give them enough lead.~~ ⑸⓿

We headed back up a north-Easterly direction to get back on our original course and never struck another trail until about eleven. We followed it until dinner time and then we stopped for a rest. We made coffee and ate some vienna sausage sandwiches and some oranges which we had brought along as something to keep us going. ⑸

We then picked up the trail again and it took a winding, zig-zag direction ~~easterly direction~~. The trail we were following ~~~~ ~~~~ ~~it was~~ I was getting fresher all the time. We came to a big Palmetto island about 2 acres with several big cypress heads in it. ~~and~~ Daddy flanked on the west and I was East of Steve and the dog. We slowly headed north, upwind, into the Palmettos and in a few minutes Steve fired and shouts at me. I turned and looked and there was the deer about 40 yards away taking flying leaps. He really looked like a great monarch with those big ant held erect and his white tail sticking up and waving ~~in~~ like a flag in a frightened, defiant sort of way. I raise my 12 guage double-barrel shot gun to my shoulder and took careful aim and fired twice but the deer ran on.

Steve told me, "Son if you can't do any better than that you'll never kill a deer." Then I told him that when I shot I saw the deer's tail fall even though he ran on. So we went over where the deer had run and we saw blood and foam on the Palmettos. So I had hit him after all.

The dog picked up the trail and we followed it for about a quarter of a mile and there the deer lay and was he a big one. He was a 10 point buck — a real "gran' daddy" and I had killed him using ~~no. 4 buck shot and only hit him with one pellet.~~ ~~I field ... him with only one pellet of no. 4 buck shot.~~

He weighed about 190 ~~pounds~~ ~~field dressed but~~ we we carrying him back to camp, and camp was four miles away ~~so before we got there~~ he became pretty heavy. He dressed out 155 pounds of the best venison in the whole world and next day it made the best christmas dinner I ever ate.

Made in the
USA
Lexington, KY